SLAY YOUR FINANCIAL GIANTS

Expert Press
www.ExpertPress.net

SLAY YOUR FINANCIAL GIANTS
Craft Your HERO Plan and Stand Strong

ISBN (paperback): 978-1-956220-92-6
ISBN (hardback): 978-1-964046-04-4

Editing by Amy Hammond
Copyediting by Hannah Skaggs
Proofreading by Geena Barret
Text design and composition by Emily Fritz
Cover design by Casey Fritz

SLAY YOUR FINANCIAL GIANTS

Craft Your HERO Plan and Stand Strong

Trent Benedetti

DEDICATION

This book—linking faith and Biblical teaching on finance with Main Steet financial wisdom—is written for the common folks who toil every day on their economic journey toward financial independence. The book has been over ten years in the making, since I first got the idea to write about faith and finance. I must thank my family: my kids, John, Christie, Michael, and Sarah—and especially my wife, Barbara—who were without their father and husband for many hours as I attended workshops, seminars, and continuing education, leaving them home alone.

Along the way, I am grateful to the programs that led me on this parallel journey of spiritual teaching—Jerusalem's way and the world way, or Main Street Investing and Finance—since most of my clients would be classified as Main Street families and businesses on their financial independence journey. I must recognize and thank the individuals and programs that have had the greatest impact on me. Among them are Dave Ramsey, both Financial Peace University and Counselor Training; Larry Burkett's Christian Financial Concepts Counselor Training; Howard Dayton's Crown Ministries Leader Training; Ron Blue's Kingdom Advisors; Mark Matson for introducing me to academic investing and modern portfolio theory; Efficient Advisors and their whole team of leaders and trainers, and Mark J. Kohler's Main Street Tax Professional Program. Kohler's Financial Ten Commandments and Trifecta were most inspirational in my own version of the Financial Ten Commandments and the HERO Plan. Kingdom Advisors Training was the basis for many of the concepts, too.

I could not have come this far without mentioning two of my college professors of Biblical theology whose influence was profound in my understanding of sacred scripture. Thank you, Michael Barber and John Kincaid, for being the best version of yourselves in passing on your knowledge of scripture to your students. And gratitude must be given to God for granting me the grace and abilities to publish over forty years of working knowledge gained in the financial field.

CONTENTS

PROLOGUE

The Biblical Wisdom of David, Solomon, and Wealth Creation

A Message from Trent Benedetti

Throughout my forty-plus years as a financial advisor and accountant, I have dealt extensively with people stressed about finances. At the beginning of my career, I included myself in that group. I lost nearly $5,000 trusting my first stockbroker. He was the expert; how could he be wrong? That failure sparked a journey whose culmination I'm thrilled to share with you. Along the way, through examining Biblical wisdom as well as Main Street education, I learned to slay financial giants. I'm here to show you how to do the same.

After that $5,000 disappeared, I felt resolute. I could be wiser than that stockbroker, I decided. I would be a financial guru and outperform—for both my clients and myself—the average advisor or Wall Street suit. I pursued standard investment education, and my walls soon displayed the certificates to prove my labors: five security licenses and designations

of CPA, CFP, investment advisor, and more showcased my prowess. Surely my clients would now be hugely prosperous!

Spoiler alert: I enjoyed some wins, but those clients still lost money in the stock market bubbles and crashes of 2000–2002 and 2007–2009. I was bewildered. Why weren't my education and Wall Street Way of advising working?

That's when I began to consider what God, faith, and philosophy say about this wealth-building journey. My faith serves as a compass for so much of my life. Why not use it to point me toward financial success? I wondered what the word of God might share about the subject and what I could learn from Main Street versus Wall Street giants.

By understanding modern economic science (Main Street, which is largely ignored in social media, television, Wall Street, and the mainstream media) and coupling it with lessons from the Bible, I share here how to find financial peace, happiness, and independence through creating your HERO Plan, which makes you the protagonist in your life story. More on that soon.

The Wall Street Way is a road full of potholes and sudden dead ends. I welcome you to instead take advice from the Bible and Main Street giants. Clear the debris from your path to win like David, who vanquished a worthy opponent with a simple slinger weapon and a clear shot at success. Let's begin.

Jerusalem Meets Main Street

Old doesn't mean wrong. Ancient wisdom is often not antiquated advice. Throughout all our evolution over the years, people have remained basically the same. We possess the same base desires, needs, and passions. Our ancestors strove for mastery and pondered the meaning of life. Sounds familiar, doesn't it?

Take Tertullian's quote, for instance: "What has Jerusalem to do with Athens, the Church with the Academy, the Christian with the heretic?" Found in *Prescription against Heretics*, these words date back to between AD 150–220. The expression is seen as an admittance of the divide between theology and philosophy, implying that they are different. Still, both the philosopher and the Christian seek truth. One looks for it in the realm of God; the other finds it within human reason. By searching on both sides, perhaps we can find the true solution somewhere in the middle.

It's no accident that the word *philosophy* is derived from the Greek *philosophia*, meaning "love of wisdom." *Theology* comes from *theos* (God) and *logos* (study), so theology is the study of God. Philosophers are scholars who think about the world, put forth arguments, and debate to better understand life and the reasons people behave the way they do. By taking Main Street philosophy into account and simultaneously considering Biblical tenets, we can learn much about life.

What Has Jerusalem to Do with Main Street Finance?

The short answer is plenty. Biblical verses accompany modern Main Street concepts throughout this book because they are so often synergistic.

Years ago, I felt a calling to become a Christian financial counselor, I sought out programs that would increase my knowledge and understanding of money and finance from a Biblical perspective. I attended Larry Burkett's Christian Financial Concepts training, and it immediately registered.

Larry's course was the first of a slew of faith-based training I embraced wholeheartedly, but my wife Barbara was skeptical. She wouldn't participate even though I would come home from these trainings full of hope for the future. We felt at an impasse. Then a multimillionaire client of mine whom I also counted as a friend said he would talk to her about attending his event. At the time, he led Dave Ramsey's Financial Peace University (FPU) class.

Barbara agreed to give it a shot. The timing wasn't great; in the middle of tax season, we drove thirty minutes each way every Thursday to the sessions. It was time well spent because what we learned would become the basis of how we treat finances as a couple. Over a cup of coffee afterward at the local McDonald's, we rehashed that night's lesson. Finally, we were on the same page with our life plan, and it was exciting! One evening, I finally asked her the question that had been gnawing at me for weeks: why had she never attended those other programs? She'd been so hesitant. They were taught by excellent men and contained much of the Biblical wisdom we encountered at FPU.

She reluctantly answered that she didn't want to be controlled and she feared the classes would lead to exactly that. Paying the bills and making the household budget gave her joy, she said. Taking that away was akin to stripping away her strengths and leaving her at the mercy of some strict advice. She would be powerless; she would be unhappy. If the classes advised this, she was not going to be on board.

I reassured her then, as I do now, that we are a team of equals. FPU taught us to understand each other's personality style and to work with each of our strengths. I see the bigger picture in life while she pays closer attention to immediate details. Taking the tasks away that brought her joy made no sense. She has a God-given talent for completing them. Why would we completely revamp our natural inclinations? That seemed unwise, to say the least.

Once we were both all-in with FPU, Barbara and I set off on a journey that has led to the book you hold in your hands. It wasn't easy and it wasn't always intuitive, but we've learned many lessons along the way. Hopefully, by reading about our experience, you'll be able to avoid some of our mistakes. These pages are a dream made tangible from my experiences with accounting and financial planning that span decades. My clients are often on similar paths of debt struggles and financial striving; they, like Barbara, often confess their fear of the unknown. I'm here to tell you that there is a way forward.

This book will present ideas and solutions to such conundrums as debt and wealth-creation vehicles. If you really struggle to understand or implement the ideas I put forth, consider enrolling in FPU. Dave Ramsey and his team give their students the tools and education necessary to embark on a financial journey with eyes wide open. Once I completed that course, I could never be blind on my wealth-building journey again. There were specific tenets I would continue to live by to give glory to God and simultaneously fill the family coffers. On the way, I would also endeavor to help my fellow man.

Along with wisdom from the Biblical hard-hitters David and Solomon, you may recognize the words of great financial teachers quoted within these pages. Besides Dave Ramsey, you'll hear from Larry Burkett, Ron Blue, Mark Kohler, and others. Throughout this amalgamation of Biblical and Main Street wisdom, I charge you to develop a bigger picture of wealth building, wealth management, and estate planning.

My prayer is that this book will lead you to systematically develop your own HERO Plan. What does that acronym stand for? I thought you'd never ask.

- **Holdings:** Enjoy your time and freedom through passive income creation.
- **Eliminate:** Reductive debt that holds you back from increasing your holdings and reduces your net worth.
- **Revocable living trust:** Establish this legal vehicle to pass on your wealth and care for those who survive you.
- **Operations:** Here, you'll find active income creation—your job and W-2 earnings. Learn to set up the businesses you run, own, or manage that create your holdings.

Beginning in chapter 1, we'll take a closer look at sound wealth-building habits as they are found in the Bible. We'll follow along with plenty of Jerusalem examples and use a smattering of Main Street insight with the Financial Ten Commandments as a guide.

CHAPTER 1

Biblical Principles and the Financial Ten Commandments

Meet the book's two main Biblical protagonists: King David and King Solomon. Note that I attribute the Jerusalem point of view primarily to King David from the Book of Psalms, and I quote his son, King Solomon, primarily from Proverbs. Yes, one could argue that the entire Bible is full of God's wisdom, as it shares with humanity how to live fully and abundantly. However, I've chosen to limit our discussions to Old Testament sayings. I encourage you to explore your own journey further in the pages of the Bible as you pursue financial independence. This, my friends, is *my* initial route.

King David

In the process of unseating King Saul from the throne of Israel, the prophet Samuel described David as a man after God's own heart. "You have done a foolish thing," Samuel said. "You have not kept the command the Lord your God gave you; if you had, he would have established your kingdom

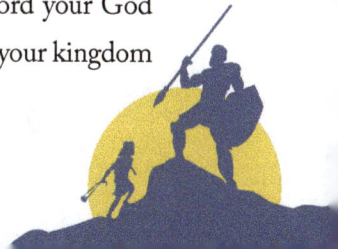

over Israel for all time. But now your kingdom will not endure; the Lord has sought out a man after his own heart and appointed him ruler of his people, because you have not kept the Lord's command" (1 Samuel 13:13–14).

David was blessed by God with a set of weapons and tools, and with one of these, he defeated one of Israel's greatest threats: the Philistine warrior Goliath. Most know the story of this giant, who serves as a metaphor for seeming impossibility. Fear gripped the army of Israel. David, a shepherd boy from Bethlehem, stepped forward to save the day. It was the slingshot event retold around the world. How's that for the tagline of a Hollywood movie?

This story is a commonly repeated Biblical highlight, but did you know that David went on to become King David, who led Israel to a great period of prosperity and wealth creation? David never lost sight of God and his relationship with him. And he didn't keep his wisdom to himself—he is credited with writing many psalms and sharing his experiences with generations. Throughout David's writings, we notice a practical and moral wisdom (in Hebrew, *hokmah*) that teaches not just how to do things but also how to make sound judgments regarding how to live life and gain happiness. This happiness can be extended to you, your family, and your community.

Meditating on the wisdom in the Book of Psalms, Proverbs, and other sacred scripture is a way to meditate on how God created us to live: "Blessed is the one who does not walk in step with the wicked or stand in the way that sinners take or sit in the company of mockers, but whose delight is in the law of the Lord, and who meditates on his law day and night" (Psalm 1:1–2).

And what is the result of meditating on God's law and acting on it? It enables the person who does so to become "like a tree planted by streams of water, which yields its fruit in season and whose leaf does not wither—whatever they do prospers" (Psalm 1:3).

King Solomon

David had a son, Solomon, who continued this journey of following God's wisdom. At age twelve, Solomon declared to God that he did not need more wealth or power than he already possessed; instead, he asked for wisdom. This quote from scripture shows what people thought of his godly request:

Solomon's wisdom was greater than the wisdom of all the people of the East, and greater than all the wisdom of Egypt. He was wiser than anyone else, including Ethan the Ezrahite—wiser than Heman, Kalkol and Darda, the sons of Mahol. And his fame spread to all the surrounding nations. He spoke three thousand proverbs and his songs numbered a thousand and five ... From all nations people came to listen to Solomon's wisdom, sent by all the kings of the world, who had heard of his wisdom (1 Kings 4:30–32, 34).

When it comes to riches, Solomon is widely considered the GOAT (greatest of all time). Adjusted for inflation, his wealth was likely greater than that of Bill Gates and Warren Buffett combined. One account states his net worth was more than a trillion dollars. Basically, if you're looking to learn from the financial expert, Solomon is your man. Luckily for us, he shares his points of view abundantly in the Bible. While not all the Proverbs are attributed to King Solomon, we learn a great deal from him about the right way of living and the *hokmah* way to pursue wealth. We also learn "instruction," or discipline, words of insight and understanding.

Keep in mind that the goal of learning the instruction is not to earn a modern-day degree but to gain the tools to craft a virtuous life that leads to true happiness, peace, and contentment. As you learn to live according to this imparted wisdom that leads to a better understanding of wealth building, you will recognize how God uses the tool of the pursuit of money to move you closer to Him.

Saint Augustine

Accepted by most scholars as one of the most important figures in the ancient Western church, Saint Augustine lived and preached during the fall of the Roman Empire, which occurred in the early fifth century. In one of his sermons, he uses the human drive to pursue money to call us to love God as much as we love the green stuff: "I have nothing to add to the love with which you love. 'Love like that, and I don't want to be loved any more than that,' says God. 'I'm talking to the riff-raff, I'm speaking to the greedy: You love money; love me just as much. Of course, I'm incomparably better; but I don't want more ample love from you; love me just as much as you love money'"(Augustine 1995, 465).

If you meditate on the lengths to which we go to obtain wealth and how much of the world around us is driven by the pursuit of it, you'll realize how radical the challenge in Proverbs is for us to pursue wisdom like silver:

My son, if you accept my words and store up my commands within you, turning your ear to wisdom and applying your heart to understanding—indeed, if you call out for insight and cry aloud for understanding, and if you look for it as for silver and search for it as for hidden treasure, then you will understand the fear of the Lord and find the knowledge of God. For the Lord gives wisdom; from his mouth come knowledge and understanding. He holds success in store for the upright, he is a shield to those whose walk is blameless, for he guards the course of the just and protects the way of his faithful ones. (Proverbs 2:1–8).

The answer to building wealth is in seeking wisdom. This common assertion can be found in various world religions and writings, including Hinduism, Buddhism, ancient Egyptian culture, Greek philosophy, and many contemporary sources. I chose the Hebrew scriptures of the Old Testament—specifically the writings attributed to David and Solomon—to share wisdom in our pursuit of happiness and wealth. Interspersed throughout these golden pieces of scripture are quotes from modern teachers who also guide us toward the truth.

The Financial Ten Commandments

Here is my challenge to you: keep Jerusalem and Main Street in harmony by taking the Biblical lessons within these pages and melding them with modern insights to glean meaning. Let's first examine how these Biblical assertions inform our world and how the philosophers agree. The Financial Ten Commandments are below.

Commandment 1: Plan diligently and live below your means.

As financial teacher Dave Ramsey taught me, and as I have since taught my clients, you can increase your income or decrease your expenses. However, you'll never be able to add passive income to your future income if you don't spend less than you make. This sounds difficult to some people, but the Bible purports that it is quite instinctual: "Go to the ant, you sluggard; consider its ways and be wise! It has no commander, no overseer or ruler, yet it stores its provisions in summer and gathers its food at harvest" (Proverbs 6:6–8).

Even the lowly ant, which pays no taxes and has no oversight to speak of, allocates its resources expediently. Otherwise, it would not have food when the seasons change and its environment is blanketed in snow. Many people do have trouble living within their means. Following the rest of the financial commandments should help change this.

Commandment 2: Eliminate reductive debt.

Reductive debt reduces your net worth, and that's not a sound financial strategy for the long run. Let's look at this principle in scripture: "The wise store up choice food and olive oil, but fools gulp theirs down" (Proverbs 21:20). Fools use up their resources quickly. And let's borrow from Dave Ramsey again. He has insight into handling this particular challenge, which he calls the "debt snowball," and he offers a great tool to eliminate credit card debt, car loans, and other debt that will eat away at your net worth. You can find more information about the debt snowball at ramseysolutions.com.

Here's good news: some debt can be favorable. Productive debt increases your net worth. It's the financial return you receive by taking out a college loan, for example, whose principal doesn't exceed a year of income. The increase in salary you can demand after holding that degree is productive.

Commandment 3: Accumulate savings to increase your holdings.

Living merely to survive, as the foolish man does, does not expand your wealth. Let's look at that verse again: "The wise store up choice food and olive oil, but fools gulp theirs down" (Proverbs 21:20). The wise have stored resources.

Consuming all your W-2 earnings and money earned from other operations is a zero-sum game, and the implications are larger than your individual situation. Without savings, there would be no advancements. Progress would stagnate. The internet would not have been invented; medical diagnostics and treatments would be nonexistent. We would all, as a species, just be living to survive.

Translating this idea to your own life in the present day, an inability to accumulate savings means you won't own a house or a rental property, for instance. Most Americans do not maintain robust savings accounts. I'm here to help you create your HERO Plan and to understand that you have to get your spending in check so that you have access to savings. To do that, begin with an emergency fund.

Ramsey believes that allocating $1,000 is enough for an emergency fund; I advise my clients to consider setting aside up to $5,000. This fund saves you from getting into further debt by being there for absolute necessities. In the savings module later in this book, I'll teach you to build this fund up to perhaps three months of financial cushion. People get sick or lose their job every day. That fund is there to cushion an unexpected blow.

The opportunity fund is another strategy I'll teach you to embrace. That way, if a real estate holding or some other opportunity arises, you can take advantage of it.

Commandment 4: Use your gifts.

"Do you see someone skilled in their work? They will serve before kings; they will not serve before officials of low rank" (Proverbs 22:29).

The Main Street view is so similar to this verse. We all have gifts, our God-given talents that are meant to be shared with the world. Your job is to figure out what your best gift is. What makes you happiest? What doesn't really feel like work? We're all going to have different ways to serve others and put forth our talents.

Yes, this means some of us will have high net salaries and businesses, and others will have smaller businesses and lower numbers on their W-2s. Our goal is to be as productive as possible to care for ourselves and our families, and to create enough leftover cash flow to embrace financial independence (also known as retirement). Giving to the next generation and charities we're inclined to support is another aspect of this financial commandment.

When you create value at work and in business, you have more to invest, spend, and give away. Abundance is a good thing. We should desire free time and extra income so that we can produce more fruit and serve others better. This helps us to both physically and spiritually feed others. God has designed us this way.

Commandment 5: Choose holdings wisely.

Holdings represent future passive income. They come in various forms, and plenty of literature is available about popular types. Later in the book, we'll examine some of the lesser-known vehicles, like solo or individual 401(k)s. We'll also examine the charitable remainder trust, which I call the HERO charitable remainder trust. This vehicle is rarely taught in school or through standard financial advisor channels.

Wealth building for passive income may include tax-favored accounts, like the Roth IRA, HSA (health savings account), and Traditional IRA. Included in this category are the self-directed pension plans and mega backdoor Roth.

Rental real estate is a key holding that can offer the benefits of appreciation (capital gain treatment upon sale). This can mean passive income when you retire. Real estate can serve as a real steppingstone to other moneymaking perks, like opportunity zone credits. It also can lead to mortgage and tax deductions and cash flow as well as to 1031 exchanges.

Commandment 6: Engage in self-directed and evidence-based investing.

Learn to increase your holdings with the right tools (evidence). Just as David felled Goliath with the sling tool, you can make informed decisions too. The main point of this commandment is to do your homework. Decide which points of view you can trust, and look at the evidence that supports them. Only then should you decide to follow the path they recommend.

Commandment 7: Seek wisdom.

"Why should fools have money in hand to buy wisdom, when they are not able to understand it?" (Proverbs 17:16). Seeking wisdom in all areas of life is what many people desire—especially those who fear God. Still, what we learn can make us uncomfortable, and we don't seek out the uncomfortable willingly. The way we learn to cope with life's stressors and to move forward in our wealth-building (holdings) journey can be greatly influenced by the weapons or tools (education and insight) that guide us forward.

"The earth is the Lord's, and everything in it" (Psalm 24:1). We are simply managers of God's resources; every spending decision is a spiritual one. Building wealth is about stewardship, not ownership. That's why the saying "You can't take it with you" holds true! It's our responsibility to gain wisdom so that we can make good and godly use of wealth.

Commandment 8: Seek education.

Attend workshops and webinars. Listen to podcasts. Read books. Embrace the truism that your education is never finished. There is always something new to learn. Hopefully, you can add this book to the tools you find valuable.

Commandment 9: Develop a generous spirit.

"Honor the Lord with your wealth, with the firstfruits of all your crops; then your barns will be filled to overflowing, and your vats will brim over with new wine" (Proverbs 3:9–10).

A generous heart. It's that simple.

Commandment 10: Set up a revocable living trust and leave a legacy.

After you've built the wealth, it's time to share it. I'll show you how.

Now that I've given you a quick overview of the commandments, the following chapters will explore each one in depth.

CHAPTER 2

Planning Diligently and Living below Your Means

The psalmist set an example for us when he wrote, "Your word is a lamp for my feet, a light on my path" (Psalm 119:105). Without God's word as a guide, how do we know the way? Accordingly, without a financial plan, our wealth-building journey is just a walk in the darkness. The illuminating lesson of Financial Commandment 1 therefore begins with self-assessment. What are your blind spots? What is keeping you from the light? It's time to discover the actions that make a difference on your financial journey.

Everyone's financial trek is different. My journey toward building a thriving accounting, financial planning, and investment advisory business was a rocky one for a while because I wasn't aware of my blind spots. Isn't that the way it usually is? You don't know what you don't know. I had goals in mind, but they weren't initially written down; I had a big-picture planning personality but had a tough time focusing on the present.

I did better in my personal life. When I met my wife, I knew she would be a good partner for me. She always seemed to be doing what needed to be done *now*. We complemented each other, and still do. Such a well-rounded picture is necessary to plan for both the future and the present, the financial and the familial.

Writing my goals down in a Franklin Planner and attending Dave Ramsey's FPU course really shifted my planning mindset to an all-inclusive one. Ramsey admitted that he met some of his goals, but not all; this reminds me of a famous quote by Zig Ziglar: "If you aim at nothing, you will hit it every time." Ramsey didn't always hit the mark, and that didn't matter. The point is that he knew where he was aiming. To have peaceful contentment on this journey toward wealth production, resist the urge to make rash adjustments to your lifestyle. Instead, make informed choices.

The lesson here is to identify your own blind spots and put your plans down on paper. Go ahead—I'll wait. Know the destination you're aiming for, and you'll be apt to take appropriate steps to get there. This will shine a light on your path that shows where you should go, step-by-step. Your financial planning journey will likely be more linear than an unpredictable zig and zag from idea to idea.

The Jerusalem View

God told the prophet Isaiah, "Forget the former things; do not dwell on the past. See, I am doing a new thing! Now it springs up; do you not perceive it?" (Isaiah 43:18–19). Once you've embarked on a new path, stay true to it. You've chosen the destination; what remains is the path you'll take to get there.

The priest philosopher Thomas Aquinas urged his listeners to hold true in this philosophy as well; he also suggested that true love derives less from emotion and more from decision. According to him, love is a choice to will the good of the other. So too is the decision to look for our blind spots, admit where and when we need help, and set goals for the good of our financial health. Finding and fixing these blind spots takes effort, courage, and discipline. Thank goodness the Bible tells us how to do it. Let's look at a few more of its principles that we can use in financial planning.

"In their hearts humans plan their course, but the Lord establishes their steps" (Proverbs 16:9). Set short-term and long-term financial goals. That way, your steps lead toward something bigger than just "getting by." *But what does the Lord want me to do?* you might ask. The Proverbs give us so much insight regarding that question.

"Dishonest money dwindles away, but whoever gathers money little by little makes it grow" (Proverbs 13:11). Spend less than you earn and don't go after the next big thing.

Responsible investing that takes into account your true risk profile is much more likely to yield long-term rewards than a quick fix.

"The rich rule over the poor, and the borrower is slave to the lender" (Proverbs 22:7). Avoid the use of reductive debt.

"Whoever loves money never has enough; whoever loves wealth is never satisfied with their income. This too is meaningless" (Ecclesiastes 5:10). Avoid a lifestyle of consumption for the sake of consumption. Yes, this book focuses on how to gain financial independence. However, if you do it just so you can buy more possessions, this is a hollow aim. Providing for your family and future generations is a much richer existence and reason for wealth building.

The Main Street View

With that said, it's time to conduct an inventory of your known strengths and weaknesses. Be honest with yourself. Write down truthful answers so you have a better understanding of where you're succeeding—and where you're falling short. Tools from Main Street in the form of standardized personality tests may help uncover blind spots. Finally, ask several members of your peer group to assess your weaknesses and strengths. How can you improve?

The House of_____

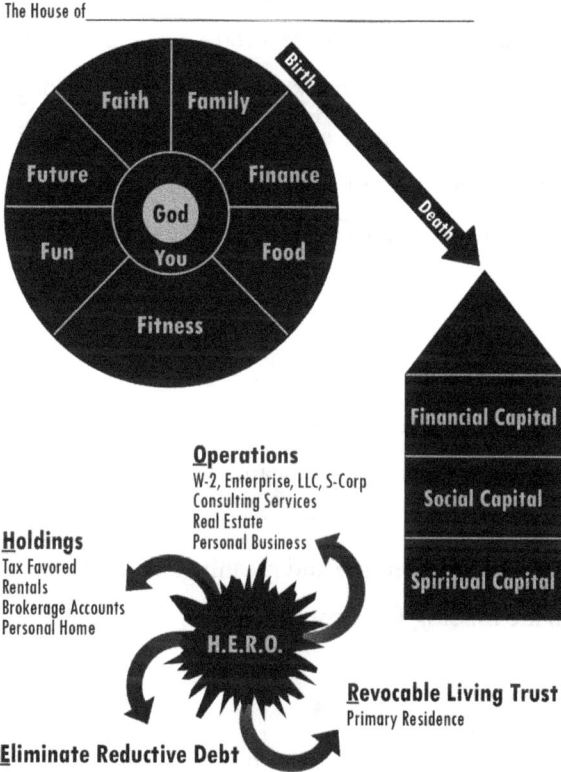

Inspired by Mark J. Kohler

Welcome to the "life balance wheel." Also called "the wheel of life" or "the coaching wheel," it goes by many names, but the aim is the same: to help those who use it assess their work and life and understand how to gain balance. Zig Ziglar, Ron Blue, and others have recommended this wheel model during coaching instruction.

The circle reminds us that life is about balance. God is at the center, and money can be used as a tool in the surrounding areas to achieve God's goals and purposes. Financial planning is largely about managing income and cash flow, but that's only a small piece of life. Here we understand that three forms of capital make up our financial lives. Of the H in the HERO Plan, holdings are the financial capital.

Financial capital

This includes money, material assets (such as real estate), and equities (such as stocks and mutual funds). It also includes personal possessions (cars, clothing, appliances, etc.) Financial capital is empty and meaningless if other forms of capital are missing from your life.

Faith capital

Knowing and having a relationship with our Creator opens us up to achieving God's goals and purposes. This relationship is developed through prayer and nurtured in a community, such as a church. I love the example that the Bible is a love letter to us. God wants us to know who he is and shares wisdom with us.

Fun/friends capital

There's no sense in developing a HERO Plan but still being miserable and unhappy in the work you do. This capital recognizes our dependence on others and our ability to choose how we interact in the world. Morality is a critical component of fun/friends capital and includes ethics. It also encompasses that good old-fashioned concept of distinguishing from right and wrong and the Golden Rule.

Now that the three forms of capital are established in your mind, it's time to set some written goals. Select your favorite pen and a piece of paper. The most effective personal and professional development tools include a written plan that contains the information you collected in commandments 1–3 from chapter 1 and identifies tasks to be completed and milestones to be achieved. Remember to make sure every goal is SMART (specific, measurable, attainable, relevant, and time-bound) and that you review tasks and milestones regularly. Quantify your progress by doing systematic checkups on a weekly, monthly, and quarterly basis.

Cash Flow Planning

"Be sure you know the condition of your flocks, give careful attention to your herds" (Proverbs 27:23). This verse lends itself so well to the concept of cash flow planning. You've likely determined by this point how much you should spend on every category of your life (fixed costs should be written down so they are easily visible). Now, it's time to monitor monthly spending. This exercise creates a short-term picture that compounds into achieving long-term goals. Traditionally, the best way to accomplish these goals is to generate a positive cash flow margin. Positive cash flow exists when you spend less than you earn, so it's time to begin controlling cash flow.

1. Basic objectives
   a. Assess your current spending habits and patterns. Different phone applications can help you keep track of daily receipts. If your twenty-five-dollar-a-week fast food habit has been on the down low, it soon won't be!
   b. Ensure your actual spending aligns with your predetermined priorities.
   c. Build liquidity so you'll be prepared for emergencies and opportunities.
   d. Take advantage of financial opportunities.

2. Cash flow control systems
   a. Create and use a budget (spending plan)—and stick to it.
   b. Identify your specific spending categories. Here's where Excel spreadsheets and QuickBooks may prove invaluable for

enterprise expenses. Consider Dave Ramsey's EveryDollar for personal household expenses. Whatever works for you to control that area, use it.

3. Envelope system
   a. Control spending on certain expenses by putting specific cash allotments in envelopes labeled for groceries, entertainment, etc. This will ensure you stay within your budget parameters.

4. Expenditure tracking
   a. Broad categories are sufficient (giving, living expenses, debt repayment, vacations, opportunity savings, etc.). Tracking allows for better control and monitoring, ensuring your spending habits match your spending priorities.

5. Lifestyle control
   a. Estimate living expenses as accurately as possible.
   b. Record the actual expenses when they become due, ensuring that your estimations are accurate.
   c. Refine the spending plan as needed.

d. Continually evaluate and revise—
    and communicate with your spouse or
    accountability partner along the way.

Financial contentment comes from spending less than you make—not from the total amount you amass. The Bible does not define an "appropriate" lifestyle. You must determine this yourself from your priorities—which need to follow your bigger HERO Plan that includes spending for your lifestyle and also for building wealth in your holdings.

The quickest way to increase margin (savings) is to decrease lifestyle costs. The second quickest way is to pad the good old-fashioned W-2 by adding a side hustle and developing it into your overall enterprise—sole proprietorship, LLC, or S corporation.

Next, let's take a deep dive into the E of the HERO Plan. Get ready to eliminate reductive debt and build your savings.

CHAPTER 3

Eliminating Reductive Debt and Building Your Savings

Let's hit the rewind button. Years ago, long before I discovered a passion for helping people plan their finances, I had a dream. That dream was a vivid one, and it didn't include a boss. I wanted to be self-employed. I was full of hope for the future. If it was just me at the helm, how could I fail? Then I started my accounting business. At the time, I had a three-year-old, an eighteen-month-old, and no clients. I also had three credit cards that got plenty of use. Over the next decade, I built that business and took as many courses as I could to improve my skill set. While I tried to increase revenue, my fiscally smart wife tried to decrease expenses the best she could.

Finally, I clawed us out of debt—and the rest, as they say, is history.

I wish I could say that's the whole truth. Here's the reality: I stopped paying attention to what it took to become debt-free in the first place, and a slow slide back into debt

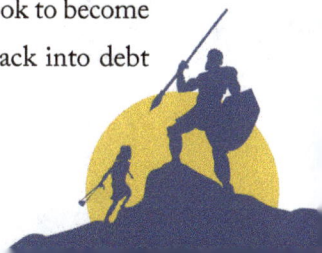

started. I began to finance and charge items yet again, not really knowing whether the return from those items would be sound. Were they good investments? I couldn't tell you. After a good deal of soul-searching, my wife and I agreed: we needed a plan. That was when I began acting on my calling to become a Christian financial counselor and seeking wisdom from both financial teachers and the Bible.

The Jerusalem View

Wait a moment, you might be thinking. Does wealth building really correlate with Biblical teachings? Well, did David vanquish Goliath? Yes! Consider the verses below that teach us what the Bible has to say about wealth and debt. They can help you with Financial Commandment 3, which is also the E of the HERO Plan: eliminate reductive debt.

"The rich rule over the poor, and the borrower is slave to the lender" (Proverbs 22:7).

"Be still before the Lord and wait patiently for him" (Psalm 37:7).

The Bible instructs us to purchase only what we can afford and to be patient. It says we should be willing to wait on God to provide for our needs within our current means; in other words, avoid borrowing to get what you want now. Don't overextend yourself. The stress that comes from not knowing whether you can ultimately afford an item will lead to unease and unrest. That's not what God wants for us.

Does this temptation to overspend on material items sound familiar? It sure does to me. I tried to succeed on my own as an entrepreneur, and in my mind, I did. Soon, though, I found myself buying items I couldn't afford. Barbara and I were sliding back into debt before we enrolled in FPU. What I learned from that class (among many other gems) is that amassing wealth is an admirable pursuit. However, slaying the financial giant we call debt demands being realistic with your assets. Can you buy that Maserati with the money in the bank, or will you have to borrow a significant amount? Does that vacation to Bali go on the credit card, or have you budgeted and saved to be able to afford it? The list goes on and on, but you get the picture.

And what about get-rich-quick schemes? The Bible has some very direct advice regarding such follies. Yes, there are exceptions to the rule (or else no one would ever win the lottery)! Still, making your long-term wealth plan hinge on a lottery ticket is not something any financial advisor would suggest. This holds true as well for investments that seem surprisingly rich. Do your homework, of course. Take the risk if you choose to. But don't expect those schemes to regularly result in high returns.

"A faithful person will be richly blessed, but one eager to get rich will not go unpunished. . . . The stingy are eager to get rich and are unaware that poverty awaits them" (Proverbs 28:20, 22). Don't borrow money to make an investment you believe will give you an immediate return *unless you have sound reasons to do so*. Remember: If it sounds too good to be true, it most likely is. Find peace with your financial decisions, not panic. Betting all your chips on one number, for example, is not a great strategy.

What about serving as a guarantor on a loan? Surely, the Good Book recommends that! You're helping your fellow man, after all. Just a moment. The Lord wants us to help our neighbors, surely, but don't pull that pocketbook out just yet. Hopefully, you're in a position to assist a family member or friend if time and circumstances line up. However, this decision demands introspection and an honest assessment of your financial status.

"Do not be one who shakes hands in pledge or puts up security for debts; if you lack the means to pay, your very bed will be snatched from under you" (Proverbs 22:26–27). Guaranteeing another person's loan is the same as taking the debt on yourself. Another example rings true here, and it's one that is decidedly modern. During a preflight safety demonstration, the flight attendant always directs passengers to apply their own oxygen mask before helping others. Take care of yourself first, and you'll then be able to take care of your children, your friends, humanity, etc. If you wound yourself financially, you will not be able to assist those in need. What's more, you may find yourself in a struggle for financial independence because of it.

Similarly, consider whether borrowing money limits your ability to be obedient to God. Yes, he wants you to help others, but he also cares about your well-being. Therefore, ask yourself: do you have the freedom before God to take on this or that debt? Borrowing does presume a future that you have envisioned, and it may deny God the opportunity to work in your life.

Does all this mean, then, that you should never incur debt? Should we all stay content with our current cash flow and not hope for better, more stable horizons? No. God wants us to succeed and to help our fellow man while we're at it. That means being more informed about our money: where it comes from, how we're growing it, and what we hope to do with our riches in the future.

The Main Street View

The way Biblical teachings advise us about taking care of ourselves so that we can best take care of others jibes with Main Street's assessment of the situation. A national study of millionaires unveils the truth that high-net-worth individuals typically avoid debt as compared with the general population. Look closer at the data, though, to unfurl an even more specific picture. Millionaires don't just avoid taking on debt altogether. They keep away from *reductive* debt as much as possible.

There's a huge difference between reductive and productive debt, though Dave Ramsey teaches that neither is favorable. This no-way view of debt is where Mr. Ramsey and I part company. Productive debt can increase your net worth, and it can be leveraged intelligently if you know how to do so. Proper planning can give you the freedom to make that choice for yourself.

Intelligent leverage begins with having enough money to cover basic costs. Once you achieve that, you can give time and energy to higher horizons, like investments—which may mean taking on carefully considered reductive debt. Consider Maslow's hierarchy of needs a solid picture of this. When the basic needs of food, shelter, and safety aren't met, no one is talking about real estate investments. It's when we're able to realize our basic needs that we're able to aim higher, toward the self-actualization and cash flow that can help not only us but others.

Here's a prime example of achieving basic needs first and then moving cautiously to gain wealth. I know a self-made millionaire who kept adding one house a year to her portfolio until she became very wealthy. The key to her strategy, she shared, was to have enough cash reserves to handle unexpected situations. For her, that reserve was (at minimum) 30 percent down on a house plus at least three to six months of mortgage payments. By always keeping those reserves at the ready, she was able to weather real estate storms and keep growing year after year. She anticipated potential setbacks and was able to avoid overextending herself.

Still not convinced? The data doesn't lie. As you'll see in the Ramsey study of millionaires and debt, they do carry productive debt. What debt they do have is incurred like my self-made millionaire friend's fund. She makes educated decisions regarding the amount of emergency money she will need to maintain throughout her wealth journey. Let's learn more about the millionaire mindset and see how much we have in common with this way of thinking.

We'll examine the five main types of borrowing before tackling any further questions about "good" versus "bad" debt.

1. Credit card

2. Consumer (cars, furniture, etc.)

3. Real estate mortgage

4. Business

5. Investments

If you guessed that numbers one and two fall in the bad (reductive) debt category, congrats! You're correct. These two do not increase your net worth. Yes, you may earn some cash back on a credit card, but if you overextend yourself and end up paying interest on the payments, that's going to be unfavorable. Conversely, debt types three, four, and five can be

SLAY YOUR FINANCIAL GIANTS

good (productive) debt in certain cases. They have the power to increase your net worth, and here's how that can happen.

Good debt comes in the form of loans, a mortgage, or lines of credit that you can use as a business owner or investor to buy real estate, expand business operations, and, within a reasonable estimation, bring in returns to surpass the debt and the cost of interest. Whew—try saying that aloud in one breath! This type of debt is not thrown away on consumer goods that do not appreciate. It represents thoughtful, productive investment.

This is the type of debt that works for you, not against you. Productive debt also includes the mortgage you use to buy your primary residence or a rental property that creates cash flow. Leveraging this debt is not negative if it can create wealth without creating too much risk in the process. Yes, there is always a risk one takes when assuming debt, no matter the kind. But using some money to grow even more money can really yield returns in the right situations.

So why is reductive debt so dangerous? Doesn't everyone deserve to buy nice things that don't necessarily lead to more cash flow? Well, yes. And also no. If you have ample cash in the coffers to cover that mega yacht and have considered the pros and cons of using that money, go for it. Just remember: a yacht can't be used to grow your business or wealth. This money isn't working for you in any productive way.

Typically, reductive debt is used to buy items you can't truly afford; when that happens, nothing good arises. That's not to say you can't have nice things. Living like a pauper is not the goal here. It's just a reminder of what's most important, and that is financial security.

This lesson is not being embraced in a widespread manner by American society. For a quick snapshot of how the general population tends to overwhelmingly use reductive debt versus millionaires, take a look at the following Ramsey study (Ramsey 2021).

Percentage of Americans Who
Currently Hold Various Types of Debt

Type of Debt	General Population	Millionaires
Credit card debt	40%	6%
Auto loan	35%	18%
Student loan	22%	2%
Medical debt	12%	2%
Family/friend loan	8%	1%

But with productive debt, we see little difference between the general population and millionaires:

Type of Debt	General Population	Millionaires
Business loan	2%	2%
Home equity loan	10%	9%
Mortgage loan	30%	34%

This study also tells us which wealth-building vehicles millionaires use the most:

Investing (employer-sponsored 401(k), Roth IRA)	80%
Investing (outside of employer: ETFs, single stock, IRA)	74%
Savings	73%
Real estate	36%
Note: Only 22% inherited their millionaire status.	

Be honest with yourself when taking on debt. Is it economically productive? Does the debt have an opportunity to increase your net worth within reasonable risk? Is it too leveraged?

If you're on a plan to eliminate reductive debt, keep making inroads. That debt will only decrease your net worth. If you're not, you may find yourself stuck in a seemingly never-ending cycle of spend, spend, spend ... and not enough save, save, save.

With all this information to digest, how does one decide which debt to incur? Don't feel as if you can never spend your hard-earned money. Here's a cheat phrase that can keep you from making subpar decisions: borrow only for economically productive purposes. Climb, crawl, or jump your way out of car loans and credit card debt, and do so as soon as possible. Based on my experience with FPU, this was the hardest step because it demands a change in lifestyle.

Once you've made the right decisions to cut debt, eventually you'll free up the cash necessary to follow Commandment 3: you'll be able to save more and to implement your savings in more productive ways. Yes, it's tough saying no to that vacation you might have otherwise put on the credit card, or the boat that your bonus doesn't cover. Saving is a habit, though, and according to the Bible, it's one that wise people embrace. It also gets easier when you realize you're working toward an ultimate goal.

"The wise store up choice food and olive oil, but fools gulp theirs down" (Proverbs 21:20). Saving implies the existence of a kind of morality. The willingness to consume less than one earns definitely does require restraint, at the very least. It's not a widespread modern phenomenon at all. Madison Avenue bombards America with advertising messages telling us to buy more, spend more. Celebrities hawk watches that only they seem to be able to afford. Designer clothes imply status (and, for some, impending bankruptcy).

It's easy to blame advertising for our shortcomings in the savings department, but all purchases are the actions of rational creatures who have free will. That's us! Too much stuff makes us want . . . more stuff. Let's not define ourselves by what we have but by what we do. William Luckey captures this sentiment in paraphrasing Pope John Paul II Encyclical, *Centesimus Annus*, no. 36, "In the eyes of the materialist-consumerist, the more I have, the better I am" (Luckey 2017). This is not the approach to money that we're striving for. Instead, we need to recognize that we have higher goals and that we are accountable for whether we reach them.

There is a multitude of motivations to save for that proverbial rainy day. It's so easy to pull out the credit card, but what about the satisfaction of achieving a return on money in the form of interest, dividends, and capital gains? Even maintaining a current standard of life hinges on expedient saving. An emergency fund to cover unexpected medical bills is imperative for peace of mind.

So what is the right way to save? This is a personal choice. My advice is to make a goal to save regardless of the return. Put that money where the principal is protected and liquid so you can access it easily if needed. Determine your own lifestyle wants and needs and use savings to achieve those goals.

One of the more strategic ways to save is by adding to your own opportunity fund, which you in turn use to purchase holdings that result in even more income. This is part of the HERO Plan and is a key to financial independence. Saving for a rental house or for a down payment on your future home and doing so in tax-deferred vehicles, such as a Roth IRA, 401(k), or SIMPLE IRA, for the passive income they provide is wise. These will create cash flow for you whether you work or not. Imagine that: making money without lifting a finger! The best investments do that minute by minute, day by day, and all because a particular investor did their research and chose the holding wisely. That particular investor can be you.

Building Your Savings

QUICK START EMERGENCY
$1,000–$5,000

Implement a Debt Snowball If Needed

PERMANENT EMERGENCY FUND
PLUS REPLACE BIG-TICKET
ITEMS FUND
(cars, vacations, etc.)
3 Months of Living Expenses
(Safety Net)

INCREASE HOLDINGS FUND
(house, deferred savings—IRA, 401(k),
ROTH, rentals, etc.)
Investment Opportunities

Thus far, we've laid the foundation for the HERO Plan. Since we've made a plan to live within your means and eliminate your reductive debt, it's now time to focus on the O in HERO. Welcome to the world of possibility that is operations!

CHAPTER 4

Applying Your Strengths to Earn More

This chapter is dedicated to helping you fulfill Commandment 4: discover your strengths and extend them to your money-making operations. What innate skills and talents do you have that can provide goods and/or services to humankind? Your operations are a result of this particular passion. They lead to the W-2 income, LLCs, and other enterprises that provide the cash flow you need to fund faith, fun, family, and any other life categories you find important. Truly, operations help you to finance what is good in life. They provide the source for cash flow and the basis for future opportunities (which then become part of your other operations). It's a symbiotic circle.

A key point to remember throughout this chapter is that more money does not naturally mean more wisdom, but wisdom may *result* in money. If you have a natural affinity for something, by the way, that may be your wisdom. It's what you were put on this planet to do.

"The blessing of the Lord brings wealth, without painful toil for it" (Proverbs 10:22). How admirable is it to embark on a wealth-building journey? Jerusalem's view of operations and moneymaking is made clear by the above Proverb. Christians in particular tend to have a complicated relationship with moneymaking. If you feel guilty about making more money, stop feeling that way—and stop that yesterday. Instead, replace that emotion with gratitude.

"Though your riches increase, do not set your heart on them" (Psalm 62:10). Through the right perspective and with the correct intentions, the endeavor of moneymaking is a blessing. Though we are not "setting our hearts" on riches, we are leaving ourselves open to being blessed by them. There's a marked difference, and the Bible teaches us as much.

Being thankful is appropriate; sharing our blessings with others is advised. Seeking wealth above all is not. With that in mind, let's dig deeper into operations, which can be your W-2 wage, a proprietorship, or a business venture. The exact endeavor will vary by individual and talent. What operation will make *you* prosperous? Likely, it's something that enlists your God-given gifts. What has been encoded in your DNA that best allows you to flourish?

Ask any teenager what they want to do for work, and the answers are all over the place. This one wants to be a stockbroker on Wall Street. He's heard that stockbrokers make a lot of money, and he wants to help other people do that—and also, he would like to be able to afford a house in the Hamptons.

Another is thinking about teaching. It's a noble profession, after all, and she really does do well with children.

Then there's the techie kid who spends hours on video games and just knows he's on this earth to develop the next generation of artificial intelligence.

Which one is correct? If the kids all have passion for their work, every single one of them is. It's the work that's undertaken just to make money that doesn't harness innate wisdom. Using one's God-given talents and gifts to help others is really what we're designed to do. Also, even though it may take that teacher more time to build a financial cushion, it's entirely possible to do so.

That's not to say that discovering one's God-given path is always easy. I'm a prime example of this. Being a financial guru wasn't what I intended to do with my life. I was going to be a biology teacher. That was the path I was on for years, but I kept getting mediocre grades and wondering why the subject seemed so difficult.

Sadly, it became apparent that teaching biology wasn't for me. Still, I felt an inner drive to excel. I just wasn't sure at *what*. Then I took an accounting class, and it felt as if I was lit from inside. This was so interesting! I couldn't wait to learn more. From that point onward, I tried to figure out what God had in store for me. Ultimately, my interest in accounting led to the discovery that I also loved financial planning.

What about you? It's time to discover work, business, and cash flow opportunities for *your* HERO journey. To do so, let's examine the O for operations more thoroughly.

The type of operations you choose to tackle should elicit in you a state of being that is positive. Work may sometimes be a struggle, but more often it should be a natural joy. The Greeks called this phenomenon *eudaimonia*, which is translated as "the fullest and purest expression of you in your most elevated state." It's also commonly referred to as a "flow state." Each of us has a spirit, or *daimon*, that embodies our greatest and most unique possibilities, and in that flow state, we find what we are meant to do.

When you find that spirit, you become the most productive, generous, resilient, innovative *you*. Whether we call it love of work or *eudaimonia*, this is the state in which you're going to be the most successful. Here, you'll have the most authentic relationship with the world. This doesn't always mean you have to be self-employed, by the way, though I do believe that's a good place to be. Being in control of your own destiny as an entrepreneur gives you the ability to navigate your efforts as you see fit.

All of this directly translates to the subject of wealth building, and it doesn't take a lucrative job to achieve it. Dave Ramsey's study *Baby Steps Millionaires: How Ordinary People*

Built Extraordinary Wealth—and How You Can Too revealed the top five jobs are engineer, accountant, teacher, manager, and attorney. Many of these people, he professed, had found their *eudaimonia*. They loved what they did. And though they were not overnight successes, they slowly and steadily built deferred compensation by investing wisely and staying out of reductive debt.

What does a millionaire look like, you ask? Here come the statistics. Of all the millionaires cited in Ramsey's study,

- 88 percent have a four-year degree;
- 62 percent graduated from public state schools, 8 percent attended community college, and 9 percent never graduated at all;
- almost half earned a B average or lower in school;
- 40 percent were involved in sports/cheerleading (the most common extracurricular activity);
- only 31 percent averaged $100,000 in household income per year, and only 7 percent averaged over $200,000 per year on their journey to becoming millionaires;
- 96 percent enjoy what they do for a career, and 64 percent say they "love" their jobs; and
- a staggering 94 percent of millionaires live on less than they make, compared with 55 percent of the general population.

Friends, let's learn from the data and take it upon ourselves to mimic the upper trajectory of wealth building these millionaires share. When your operations are in sync with your personal predilections and purpose, it's easier to stay the course.

The Jerusalem View

"Honor the Lord with your wealth, with the firstfruits of all your crops; then your barns will be filled to overflowing, and your vats will brim over with new wine" (Proverbs 3:9–10). Within this quote lies the truth of overflowing supply: What does one do with the extra money that's left over after basic expenses are met? This is an integral part of your financial management, and it's a vital one to consider. How do we flourish in our work and business ventures? How do we continue to do so? And what do we do with the surplus?

Before we answer the question of where our money should go, we must begin with an understanding of who we humans are as a species and what we are here to accomplish individually on Earth. Each of us must stay true to what God made us to do. This daily desire to please him comes from the knowledge that we are made in the image of God and that we exist for a reason. Each decision we make matters, and we should take nothing for granted. Every last choice we make can either honor God or defy his desires and bring suffering.

We are able and encouraged to be as productive with our talents as possible. In doing so, we benefit not only ourselves but others. Consider the average lifespan; we have limited time, talent, and treasure. When we spend all of the above wisely, we should naturally have more profit. The more treasure that is left over, the more we can serve others and fulfill God's desires for us.

Human: The Job Description

Can you imagine God writing a job description for humanity? Because each of us is so unique, you might think the words would vary based on the person. However, according to God, the job description for each human on Earth is the same. In Genesis 1:28–29, God helps us understand what he wants us to do:

> God blessed them and said to them, "Be fruitful and increase in number; fill the earth and subdue it. Rule over the fish in the sea and the birds in the sky and over every living creature that moves on the ground."
>
> Then God said, "I will give you every seed-bearing plant on the face of the whole earth and every tree that has fruit with seed in it. They will be yours for food. And to all the beasts of the earth and all the birds in the sky and all the creatures that move

along the ground—everything that has the breath of life in it—I give every green plant for food."

God has given us the tools we need to survive and thrive. In Genesis 2, God continues by giving us our marching orders and furthering our job description. Humans have a special role in cultivating God's creation of Earth, as we see in Genesis 2:15: "The Lord God took the man and put him in the Garden of Eden to work it and take care of it."

We are here to do two fundamental things: work the garden (Earth) and take care of it. Taking care of something requires putting work into it and protecting it from destruction. God desires us to multiply, prosper, cultivate, and enjoy his good creation. What's more, he has given us all the materials necessary to do our job well. God's intentional design of man fits perfectly into his design of all creation.

When we do what God intends us to do, we leave the planet better than when we arrived on it. This directly correlates to the HERO Plan and its goal to help you not only amass wealth and pass it on to future generations but support a charitable endeavor in the process.

Note: God created you to be *you*. It doesn't matter if you are a pastor, a janitor, or a CEO. You are the only you there is or ever has been, and success in life is found when you identify your God-given purpose and pursue mastery— just a reminder!

No Man Is an Island—Interdependence

Your work and business ventures are always going to correlate to your interdependence with humanity. From the beginning, we were made to be part of a community. We need each other because we are not God; none of us are omnipotent. We cannot do all things perfectly. Moreover, when we try completing tasks beyond our abilities, we find ourselves frustrated by our own futility. Perhaps you've said aloud something akin to "Math is not my thing" or "English was my worst subject—I just don't come by this writing thing easily." Take a deep breath and be confident in the abilities you do have. There is a reason we all possess different aptitudes and mastery.

This is not to say we shouldn't try mastering new skills, but it does reveal the truth that relying on each other is a natural course of being. Our finite, limited design requires us to enter trading relationships—and that's natural! Our businesses provide goods and services (our investments), whether those are rentals or the markets (equity and fixed), to support others.

Even in our own homes, one person may be better at paying bills, while another thrives at thrifty grocery shopping. Remember how my wife likes to make the budget? She's great at it. When we can allocate the workload based on our strengths, we can profit more. When we profit more, we can serve others and honor God.

To bring this constant circle into words, the Old Testament puts forth a concept called *shalom*. Shalom is the universal understanding that all things are interdependent, that they work and flourish together. When we embrace this state of being, we experience a kind of peace that passes all understanding. Shalom is what I hope for you in your operations. Be true to yourself regarding your strengths, and enlist others to help with the weaknesses. Together, you'll all thrive!

The Main Street View

Like Jerusalem, Main Street also has a lot to say about our talents and abilities. "No man is an island," declared the writer John Donne. Well said, Mr. Donne: We can't be all things to all people, and we depend on each other to thrive in this world. Specialization, the popular view purports, is simply the way we are each made to live. This philosophy is a win for the world, as it points out that we must rely on each other.

We see this echoed in the words of Adam Smith, the eighteenth-century Scottish philosopher who explained the concept of division of labor as stemming from human reason. It just makes sense, he believed, that we bring all of our talents together to make one great outcome and do that over and over again.

"This division of labour," he said, "from which so many advantages are derived, is not originally the effect of any human wisdom, which foresees and intends that general opulence to which it gives occasion. It is the necessary, though very slow and gradual, consequence of a certain propensity in human nature which has in view no such extensive utility; the propensity to truck, barter, and exchange one thing for another" (Smith 2003, 22).

Though not an economist, Smith was a professor of moral philosophy. He wrote *An Inquiry into the Nature and Causes of the Wealth of Nations* because he considered the state-run economy of mercantilism, which sought to increase the prosperity and power of a nation through restrictive trade practices and increased domestic employment, to be preposterous. Mercantilism was the economic system in operation during Smith's life, and he viewed it as not only inefficient but also immoral. The practice made most people poor and rulers extremely rich. Trade was extremely misshapen. Progress was difficult because unless you could do everything, you likely had a nearly impossible time being efficient in your daily life.

As we begin to trade more and more of our special skills and gather money in the process, we begin to store excess funds as capital to use later. We then spend this to better our own lives, and subsequently those of the people with whom we exchange money. Their families end up with a better quality of life as well. Do you see the cycle here? When people consider how their efforts intrinsically help others earn money and security as well, it becomes much easier to convince them that wealth building is a worthy endeavor.

Your wealth-creation journey is a reminder that all social interaction depends on the actions of individuals. The so-called system you operate within, whether you have a W-2 job or own a business, depends on interaction with others as free agents. Aristotle tells us that all men act with an end in mind. The goal for which they act is based on what they value. That goal is universal: people act to better their own lives and the lives of those they hold dear.

Is this inherently selfish? Adam Smith didn't think so. Smith helps us to understand the concept of specialization as a benefit to humanity. He fought for the right of people to flourish through free trade, which in turn led to more specialization and more individual success. When everyone is a jack-of-all-trades but a master of none, progress can't happen. It's impossible to be good at everything, no matter how hard we try!

Thanks to this concept of specialization spurring the advancement of free trade, life quickly became better than before in Smith's time. Infant mortality rates decreased. Average lifespans started to rise. Medicines were rapidly developed. Time was now spent making life better, not simply surviving—all because we were working together.

One of the reasons free trade works so well is that an impulse to strive is built into our very nature as a species. As we interact with others, we seek to benefit our self-interest. In turn, other people seek to benefit theirs. This wealth-building endeavor is truly a symbiotic act, with everyone benefiting in the process. As a species, we are truly hardwired for this. Another snippet from chapter 2 of Smith's *Wealth of Nations* declares as much:

> But man has almost constant occasion for the help of his brethren, and it is in vain for him to expect it from their benevolence only. He will be more likely to prevail if he can interest their self-love in his favour, and show them that it is for their own advantage to do for him what he requires of them. Whoever offers to another a bargain of any kind, proposes to do this. Give me that which I want, and you shall have this which you want, is the meaning of every such offer; and it is in this manner that we obtain from one another the far greater part of those good offices which we stand in need of. It is not from the benevolence of the butcher, the brewer, or the baker that we expect our dinner, but from regard to their own interest. We address ourselves, not to their humanity but to their self-love, and never talk to them of our own necessities but of their advantages.

When Smith talks of self-love, he is not talking about selfishness or greed. He uses this word in the Biblical sense as the basis to love one's neighbor as oneself. God *expects* us to love ourselves. If we didn't love ourselves, we wouldn't take care of our own physical or emotional needs. We also wouldn't take steps to please God and help our fellow humans.

Saint Thomas Aquinas, a theologian of the Middle Ages, had plenty to say about the matter. Reginald Garrigou-Lagrange explains as much in his book *The Three Ages of the Interior Life*: "St. Thomas clearly distinguishes between self-love which is blamable and that which is not ... it is indeed distinct from charity, but is not contrary thereto, as when a man loves himself from the point of view of his own good, yet not so as to place his end in this his own good" (Garrigou-Lagrange 1948).

Jerusalem and Main Street agree: A prosperous operation benefits everyone involved. Think about all the good you'll do for yourself, your family, and those you exchange money with as your W-2, LLC, side hustle, etc., flourishes. The ramifications are far-reaching—and they are far from selfish.

CHAPTER 5

Choosing Your Holdings with Care

The H of the HERO Plan is holdings (investments). Remember that story about my ill-fated $5,000 investment in a very specific stock? That debacle led me to become a collector of licenses. I was trying to decode the answer to success, and this seemed a solid way to do it. With more education, surely I'd have a better chance at decoding investment strategies. I'd learn "the secret."

I earned my first securities license in 1987 and kept amassing licenses from then on out. Then I had an epiphany: I began to notice down markets that I could offer no real explanation for, and I started developing my own ideas about outperforming the market.

The first of these down markets was back in 2001–2003. Remember the dot-com bubble? It was a very slow downward slide. The market suffered close to a 20 percent loss, which would be considered a recession. I was left feeling just as helpless when the stock market crashes of 2008 and 2009 happened. The market fell by nearly 50 percent during

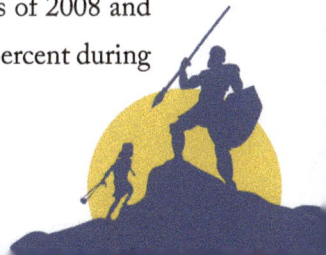

that drop. While this was not as bad as the crash of 1929, which brought nearly 90 percent losses, at least that crash took nearly four years. The 2008 crash lost 50 percent in almost eighteen months. It took nearly five years to recover from that.

Here's what we know for sure, undoubtedly and 100 percent: the market fluctuates. Reasons for the volatility vary widely, and everyone seems to have a theory. I realized a truth: no matter how much knowledge and how many licenses I amassed, there was always going to be volatility in the market. Still, even through the fluctuation, the overall trend was an upward one. What could I learn from this realization, and how could this information help my clients?

In 2011, I began learning about modern economic science—more specifically, modern portfolio theory. What I learned was humbling. Note: If you win a Nobel Prize in economic science, you're probably smarter than me. I had learned about stock picking and market timing in college, but this wasn't going to give my clients peace of mind. The practice was just too volatile. It was time to look to the experts (those aforementioned Nobel Prize winners) and, of course, to Jerusalem. Here, I believed, I'd find my answers.

The Jerusalem View

To learn how to fulfill Commandment 5, to choose your holdings wisely, let's begin with Jerusalem, and with a story that you most likely know. I bet you never thought it was a metaphor for your own wealth building! This book is about slaying your financial giants, those behemoths keeping you from whole success in life. And that sounds precisely like David versus Goliath.

The famous giant Goliath dared any man to fight him. This man was the Arnold Schwarzenegger of his army; needless to say, no one initially jumped at the challenge. The Israelites and Philistines were at an impasse on the battle-field. Finally, a shepherd boy, David, approached the king of Israel and offered his own take on the situation.

It was simple, he said. You can almost imagine him sighing at the simplicity of it all. If a bear came and carried off a member of his flock, he would go after the beast, strike it, and rescue the sheep. When the fierce animal inevitably turned on him, he would do what he had always done, which was to seize it by the hair, strike, and kill it.

This all seemed straightforward enough. As a killer of lions and bears, David believed in himself. How much fiercer could this Philistine be, after all, than the king of the jungle? How much more dangerous could he be than a hungry bear? Compared to his daily threats out on the pasture, this was a cinch.

Still, the Israelite army must have been worried when they saw David approach the giant with a simple slinger weapon. That slinger was of a design that had been around for centuries, and this wasn't some souped-up hybrid model. "Just a slingshot," people must have whispered. "How will that do anything? And he's so little!"

Hundreds of years later, experts would test the force of the slinger weapon's pebble and find it to be similar in velocity and power to that of a .357 Magnum revolver. What's more, slingers can be accurate over two hundred yards. And there was no worry about running out of ammunition. Rocks no doubt littered the battlefield.

That shepherd boy knew he had the right mindset and the right weapon. He had already discovered his unique abilities and talents, as we discussed in the last chapter. They did not extend to wielding a heavy sword; that was not natural to him. Surely, as both armies watched this boy face what seemed to be a superior adversary, they thought his chances of success were low.

We all know what happened next. Believe it: this story is a fantastic metaphor for how we approach our HERO Plan. By slaying the Wall Street giants and all the other popular opinions and behaviors that keep us from achieving our full potential, we are able to succeed. And we can do so with the weapons we amass through wisdom. Those weapons help us make the right choices and win the fight.

The Main Street View

Holdings are a prime weapon for slaying those Wall Street giants. They are the assets you own, or hold, and they can take the shape of many different vehicles: land, stocks, capital, and more. Within your operations, for example, the equity markets are one of the great weapons you can use to build up your holdings. Before we go into greater depth about that, let's see what other guidance Main Street can give us regarding directions toward success.

It doesn't matter, ultimately, what faith we belong to. If we are atheist, Islamic, Protestant, Hindu, or some other faith, it doesn't change the fact that we are interdependent. Leonard Read wrote a story about the humble pencil in 1958 that reminds us of this. He used the pencil as a universal example of a good or service that humanity provides to each other. Its components can be amassed by humans from all walks of life around the globe. Yet if we were in the same room, we might not get along. The impetus to better our economic condition is something we all have in common.

This example of the pencil demonstrates the remarkable dependence of humanity on the economic growth of the whole world. It's referred to as God's Invisible Hand, exercising his divine providence over all the goods and services we use and consume. American businessman and libertarian advocate Read published his essay "I, Pencil" in 1958. It's centuries apart from the actions of David that still resonate today. Still, both stories carry with them the weight of truth through the ages.

Consider, Read says, the globe-spanning chain of events required to produce so simple an object as a pencil. No centralized authority, he insists, could ever possess all the knowledge and skills necessary to efficiently coordinate these events. But market economies do such miracles automatically.

Hold a pencil in your hand. It looks like such a basic object. Nothing fancy here, you might think—just one of those everyday things that blend into life. Look closer, and you are transported back to its origins: a cedar tree in the Pacific Northwest, perhaps. What about the gear used to harvest those logs and the people and skill sets necessary to manufacture and employ the equipment? Read's essay takes us through the seemingly endless supply chain to illustrate how impressive even the manufacture of that one pencil is.

The logs are shipped by rail to a mill. Specialized machines fashion the logs into pencils. The "lead" core is crafted from graphite mined in Sri Lanka and mixed with Mississippi clay, Mexican candelilla wax, and various chemicals. The lacquer made from castor oil is applied, and the label imprinted using resins and carbon black. The list goes on and on.

Read's point is twofold: First, millions of human beings have had a hand in making that pencil. Second, no single individual contributed more than a certain skill set to the complex process. Because each step in the supply chain is indispensable, so too are the knowledge and skill of each worker. Each laborer's actions toward that pencil are elicited by the "Invisible Hand," a metaphor for market economics coined by Adam Smith. Smith wrote in *The Wealth of Nations* that the oil worker is motivated solely by the desire to "exchange his tiny know-how for the goods and services he needs and wants." This may or may not involve pencils!

How does this correlate to your situation as a worker? Consider the miners, loggers, and company executives. Everyone works to earn money to spend as they see fit. Others then work to supply *them* with goods and services that they procure by spending their money. There, again, is the circle that keeps turning.

People who fail to understand the interdependent logic of supply and demand often conclude that such complex coordination can be achieved only by a central authority. This, Read says, is not correct. When the government monopolizes the provision of goods and services, many citizens come to believe the private sector would be incapable of providing them efficiently. Let's give humanity some credit, please. We successfully perform much more complicated tasks than, say, the government-run mail delivery. What about the automobile and airline industries? These are run without government coercion.

This pernicious lack of faith in free people has encouraged an expansion of government control that is chipping away at society's freedom. Read argues that maintaining a free society requires widespread public understanding and acceptance of the Invisible Hand. To him, the Hand is akin to natural law. Faith in free markets is as reasonable as faith in "the sun, the rain, a cedar tree, the good earth." God's handiwork in the creation of natural law and of humans made in his image is visible in the results. Let's look next at what happens because of it.

More Evidence for the Equity Market

The equity market is really the result of operations of human wisdom and interconnectedness. It's a merging of all the specialization we examined in the last chapter and stands as a beautiful example of us coming together in harmony as a species to produce all the goods and services of the world. If this natural progression is not enough evidence for the effectiveness of the equity market, consider the examples given by Dr. Jeremy Siegel, a Wharton School of Business professor who published his sixth edition of *Stocks for the Long Run* in 2022.

Within his seminal work, Siegel examines equity markets that range back to when Thomas Jefferson was president of the United States. Through the years, he explains, the market has grown approximately 8 percent (including inflation) since 1802. He demonstrates that if you reinvest your dividends, the market outperforms long-run bonds, Treasury bills, gold, and currencies over the last two centuries.

Total Asset Returns

Total nominal return indexes, 1802–2021

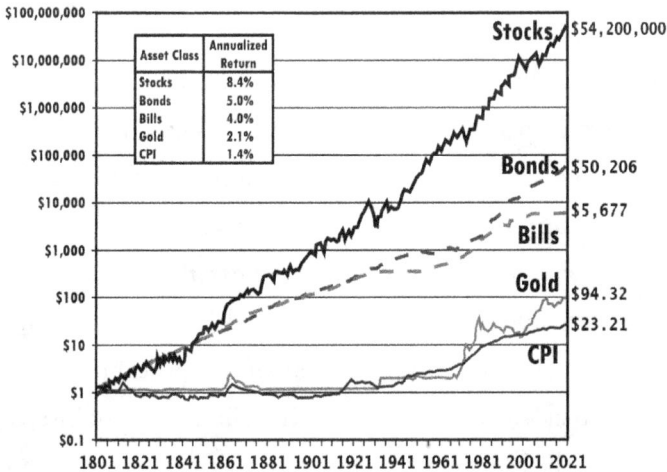

Asset Class	Annualized Return
Stocks	8.4%
Bonds	5.0%
Bills	4.0%
Gold	2.1%
CPI	1.4%

Stocks $54,200,000

Bonds $50,206

$5,677

Bills

Gold $94.32

$23.21

CPI

Source: Jeremy Siegel, "Stocks for the Long Run", 6th edition (McGraw-Hill Publishing) New York, NY 2023, 23.

One can't help looking at that graphic and wondering, Is this a market that's controlled, or is it one that's a natural progression of what humankind naturally does when free of excessive regulation? Is it that Invisible Hand trying to show us that the equity markets are in fact a fantastic place to invest in the long run? Siegel's pundits point to the fact that his data begins with just a handful of stocks, because that's all we have to track back in the early 1800s. It's true that even in the 1930s examples, his data may not be completely accurate.

With that in mind, we'll go ahead and also look at evidence that dates from 1927 to the present just to be sure we can draw an accurate picture. My main hope in using these examples is for you to understand that the specialization that increases your operational income and cash flow is the same one the graph features. It gives us this stock yield.

No investment advisor can ever guarantee that the market will repeat a trend in the next thirty years. We can't even promise the next thirty days! However, by using common sense mixed with reason and empirical evidence, we can make an educated guess. That, in this age of investments, is the best we can hope for, and it's a weapon that can help you gain wealth.

Even More Evidence for the Equity Market

In the summer of 1929, a journalist named Samuel Crowther interviewed John J. Raskob, a senior financial executive at

General Motors. Raskob had some insight as to how a typical individual could build wealth by investing in stocks, and he shared this information with gusto. Crowther published Raskob's ideas in a *Ladies' Home Journal* article entitled "Everybody Ought to Be Rich."

Raskob claimed that America was on the verge of a tremendous industrial expansion and that by putting just $15 a month into common stocks, investors could expect their wealth to steadily grow to $80,000 over the next twenty years. That's a return of 24 percent a year! The detractors scoffed. Surely, this could not be done. In the atmosphere of the 1920s bull market, it seemed even less likely. Still, seeking a quick profit, millions of people put their savings into the market.

You can probably guess what happened next. On September 3, 1929, a few days after Raskob's advice appeared, the Dow Jones Industrial Average hit a historic high of 381.17. Seven weeks later, stocks crashed. What followed for the next thirty-four months was the most devastating decline in share values in American history.

When the carnage finally stopped on July 8, 1932, the Dow Industrials stood at 41.22, and the market value of the world's greatest corporations had declined by 89 percent. The life savings of countless Americans were wiped out. Thousands of investors who had borrowed money to purchase stocks were forced into bankruptcy. America was left breathless, in shock from the deepest economic depression in the nation's history, and in a deep depression.

Understandably, Raskob's advice was ridiculed and denounced for years to come. Today, popular opinion is that it's an example of the insane notion that the market could rise forever, as well as a reminder of the foolishness of those who ignored the tremendous risks in stocks. Conventional wisdom holds that Raskob's foolhardy advice epitomizes the mania that periodically overruns Wall Street.

But is that verdict fair? The answer may surprise you. No, it's not. Over time, investing in stocks has been a winning strategy, whether one starts with such an investment plan at a market high or not. Calculate the value of the portfolio of an investor who followed Raskob's advice in 1929 (which was to patiently put $15 each month into the market), and that accumulation would exceed that of someone who placed the same money in Treasury bills after fewer than *four years.*

By 1949, the end of the twenty-year term Raskob recommended, such a person's stock portfolio would have accumulated almost $9,000, a return of 7.86 percent. That's more than double the annual return in bonds. After thirty years, the portfolio would have grown to over $60,000, with an annual return rising to 12.72 percent.

Though these returns are not as high as Raskob projected, the total return of the stock portfolio over thirty years was more than eight times the accumulation in bonds and more than nine times that in Treasury bills. Those who never bought stock because of the Great Crash found their savings to be far lower than those of investors who had patiently accumulated equity.

The story of John Raskob's much-ridiculed and much-misunderstood advice illustrates an important theme in the history of Wall Street. Bull and bear markets lead to sensational stories of incredible gains and devastating losses. However, patient stock investors who see past the scary headlines have almost always outperformed those who flee to bonds or other assets. Even such calamitous events as the 1929 stock crash, the financial crisis of 2008, and the COVID-19 pandemic have not negated the superiority of stocks as long-term investments.

Let's look further at stocks for the long run. That's what Dr. Jeremy Siegel did. In that book, his research makes a compelling case for stocks as a central part of any long-term investment strategy. Specifically, stocks are held up as a tool to protect wealth against inflation. Dr. Siegel based his case on nearly two hundred years of US market data, which reveals equities as the best-performing asset class. He stresses that the best way to grow and preserve wealth over the long run is to own a diversified portfolio of equities.

Stocks are a more volatile asset class in the short term, he says, so investors should account for that near-term volatility in their investment plans. This holds especially true for those who are nearing retirement or are recently retired. The sequence of annual investment returns can be just as important for lifetime performance as the annual returns themselves. A large drawdown early in an investment timeline can significantly impact performance over the long term.

As we end this chapter, having introduced the concept of the Invisible Hand, we will now begin to look at what to do with your holdings in chapter 6. Let's look at some examples of holdings and investigate why these equity markets may in fact be one of the best tools for you to choose. Just as the slinger weapon was the best tool for David, holdings possess the power to slay financial giants. David had to wield his weapon correctly to deliver the pebble straight and true. The same applies to your financial strategy.

CHAPTER 6

Investing: The Case against Market Timing and Security Selection

Imagine if David had been made to fight with a heavy mace instead of his simple slingshot: The story probably would have been very different. Invest with evidence as your main tool and avoid false weapons that will not bring you to victory. In this chapter, we'll take a look at the *wrong* tools that some people believe will increase their wealth and think about why we even embark on a holding strategy in the first place. Plenty of bad investing advice is shared as false gospel every day. Why do we invest, how do we do it, and how can we move that excess money somewhere that generates passive income? The answers to these questions will help you follow Commandment 6: engage in self-directed and evidence-based investing.

The Jerusalem View

There was no stock market during the time of Jesus. Can you imagine the disciples on the trading floor? What a sight that

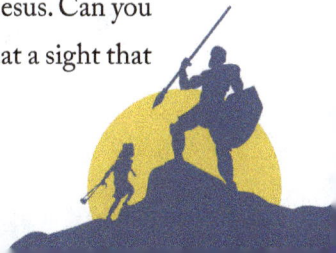

would have been: Simon Peter eagerly buying shares of New Testament companies famous for their solid moral foundations; Judas investing all his money in Enron.

No, we're spared that image in the Bible. We do see plenty of declarations in scripture about holdings, though. Storing funds you acquire during your most productive years for use later in life is logical . . . and also Biblical, as it turns out. Saving money for when you're no longer working just makes sense.

"Go to the ant, you sluggard; consider its ways and be wise! It has no commander, no overseer or ruler, yet it stores its provisions in summer and gathers its food at harvest" (Proverbs 6:6–8). This advice may be intuitive, but that doesn't mean it's always easy to follow.

The Main Street View

Madison Avenue does not necessarily want you to invest with evidence. They want you to invest in the products and services they advertise in the media. A false weapon, like the coercion accomplished by advertising, is like a cap gun. Using it is akin to shooting blanks and can ruin your long-term wealth strategy. We can narrow this down to three main problems in the niches of equity and stock investing.

The first viewpoint is that stock picking (also called security selection) can help you outperform the market. The second, which we hear quite frequently, is the concept of market timing as a means to "guesstimate" the market's future. There are people who believe they are endowed with superior wisdom who purport to know the next big thing in investing. We're missing out if we don't follow their advice. If this sounds too good to be true, that's because it is.

Finally, we have the Wall Street gurus, who compel us to chase a manager's past performance in the hopes that it was not a fluke but a sure thing, a guaranteed return.

Understanding risk, return, cost, and probability will help you invest in your long-term financial independence (retirement). Constructing and maintaining your investment strategy should consistently optimize the risks you are able to tolerate with the rewards you want, with the highest probability of success. That's a lot to remember, but it's really a wonderful equation to keep in mind. Your risk profile will be different from someone else's simply because your financial goals will be different.

What about beating the market? It's possible to figure out the ebbs and flows and to invest strategically with that mindset, right? I'm sorry to share with you that consistently beating the market is difficult, if not impossible. If a money manager could beat the market with their skill and foresight, it really would be unnecessary for them to hold a large number of stocks or mutual funds within a portfolio. This is almost never the case. Instead, what these managers do is give you a large number of products, close their eyes, and declare a silent "good luck." They cross their fingers. And it usually doesn't work.

Imagine a casino floor with a thousand roulette wheels. Someone is going to yell, "Winner!" eventually. Now, imagine those wheels are actually 50,000 stocks and 30,000 mutual funds. This is the magnitude of the choices these money managers have! They really just play a game of large numbers, knowing someone, sometime, is bound to win. And guess what? They don't talk about the losers, and they don't have a clue about how exactly to beat the market. The winner is put on a pedestal as the "normal" outcome.

Here's a look at the wrong way to invest. Let's take a peek at a Vanguard study that used Morningstar data over a fifteen-year period (Wimmer 2013). The study began with more than 1,500 mutual funds actively traded at the beginning. Fifteen years later, half of those funds had either closed or merged with other funds. There was no way to measure how many managers of the remaining funds actually just moved on to others without notice. Participants in the study ended up with multiple active managers.

Your investing timetable might be longer than fifteen years. That's why it's important to know that only 842 of those funds survived the fifteen-year period. Fewer than one out of five funds did any better than the five-year average. Maybe you're one of the lucky ones; maybe you can identify the winners. But what are the odds that anyone would both identify the winners *and* hold on to them for fifteen years? The prospect is exhausting—and near impossible.

Ultimately, the study shows that no matter which asset class or style of investment you choose, active management outperformance is typically very short-lived. In good times as well as in bad, active management has consistently produced underwhelming results. Therefore, avoid such unnecessary risks. Don't gamble when the odds are against you. Stay out of the casino of active management.

By the way, even if someone did identify in advance what would ultimately be the 275 best funds and invested in them, for example, here's the problem: during the fifteen-year period, 97 percent of the funds underperformed the benchmark. This happened during not just one year, and not just two. It happened at least five years running. The evidence is clear: active fund managers as a whole underperform their relative benchmarks over time.

The Scorecard

Since I'm so adamant that you use evidence-based investing strategies, let's examine the results of a study by S&P described in their seminal work known as the SPIVA (S&P Indexes versus Active) study. The SPIVA Scorecard Year End 2020 results show nearly a 74 percent fail by Active Funds failing to be the comparison index over a five-year period and nearly a 76 percent fail for Active Funds compared to the ten-year index (SPIVA 2021). This indicates the percentage of active managers who fail to beat their relative benchmark, regardless of how much risk they took trying to do so. Some categories are worse than others.

Simply put, your odds of finding the "superior" manager or stock picker are only about one in four. You can't identify them in advance. And regardless of asset class or style focus, active management outperformance tends to be short-lived. In good times and in bad, active management consistently shows itself to provide inconsistent results.

Let's review:

1. Beating the market before costs is a zero-sum game.

2. Beating the market after costs is a loser's game.

So how does one play this game of wealth building to win? It helps to further understand what *not* to do. Let's examine the DALBAR studies to illustrate this.

The Behavior Gap: Diversification and the Average Investor 2001-2020 (20 Years)

DALBAR is an independent firm that conducts annual studies to examine investor behavior. Their 2021 mid-year update to its QAIB report (Quantitative Analysis of Investor Behavior) gives insight into investor behavior. The QAIB report has been the nation's leading study on investor behavior for the past twenty-seven years. The report for the period ending June 30, 2021, found that the gap of returns between the Average Equity Fund Investor and the US equity market has remained consistent, with investors underperforming the market (DALBAR 2021).

The study looked at a balanced portfolio with 60 percent invested in S&P 500 Index and 40 percent invested in high-quality US fixed income, represented by the Bloomberg Barclays US Aggregate Index. The portfolio is rebalanced annually. Average cost allocation investor return is based on an analysis of DALBAR investor behavior.

Imagine it: An investor takes $100,000 at the beginning of a twenty-year period and has a portfolio of 60 percent equities and 40 percent fixed. This doesn't include management fees or expenses. In this hypothetical illustration (and this is pretty consistent year after year), the portfolio grows to nearly $350,000 (about 6.4 percent). The average investor, though, doesn't achieve that. They instead earn less than 3 percent.

There is a big difference between investor behavior and the results actual market indexes achieve. What are some of the reasons for this behavior gap? The graphic, Investor Conflicts, illustrates we are not irrational. But we tend to be emotional and human. We do have mental conflicts that affect our choices. Investing is SIMPLE . . . but doing it well is not EASY.

Investor Conflicts

Anchoring
Relating to the familiar experiences, even when inapproppriate

Diversification
Seeking to reduce risk, but simply using different sources.

Optimism
Belief that good things happen to me and bad things to others

Mental Accounting
Taking undue risk in one area and avoiding rational risk in another

Media Response
Tendency to react to news without reasonable examination

Narrow Framing
Making decisions without considering all implications

Regret
Treating errors of commission more seriously than errors of omission

Loss Aversion
Expecting to find high returns with low risk

Herding
Copying the behavior of others even in the face of unfavorable outcomes

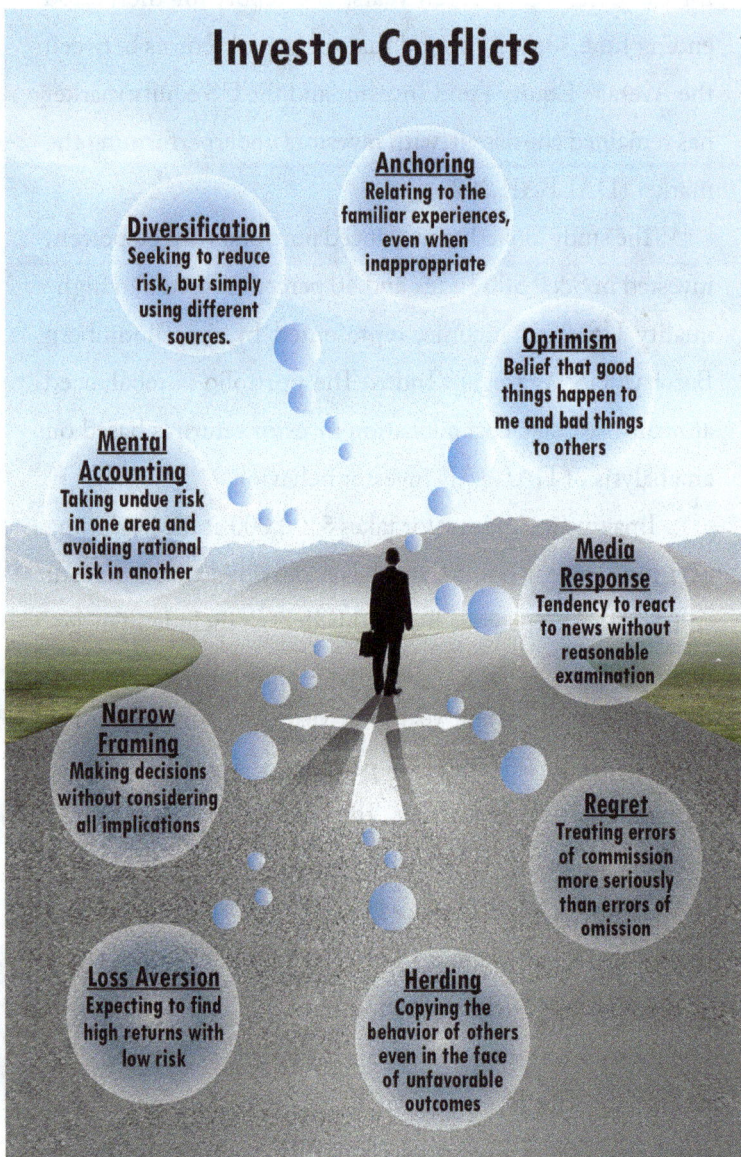

This seems perplexing. If we know the right actions to take, why are we not taking them? This question is so widespread that behavior statistics is one of the largest growing fields in economic investing science. It's also stark evidence that if you continue to subscribe to what the Wall Street gurus say is truth, you will destroy your ability to create and grow your holdings.

With that said, stay away from stock picking. Resist the urge to find patterns where there may be none. Leave market timing to the clocks ticking on the stock exchange. Do not follow financial gurus who purport to know all the answers when it comes to the above. Instead, pivot to the Jerusalem way to deduce the right tool and weapon behavior.

Let's examine a psalm from King David and one of Solomon's proverbs. Psalm 46 gives us words for times of trouble; they are prayers to reach out beyond yourself, to God: "God is our refuge and strength, an ever-present help in trouble. Therefore we will not fear, though the earth give way and the mountains fall into the heart of the sea, though its waters roar and foam and the mountains quake with their surging" (Psalm 46:1–3).

Instead of chasing what the Wall Street gurus say is the next star stock, I recommend the Solomon Strategy. Slow and steady wins the race, as they say, and patience rules the day. Those who are caught up in the lies of the investment industry find themselves sapped of energy and money.

Following stock picking and the next "big" money manager is exhausting and often unproductive. Take a deep breath and trust in the process.

God wants the best for us. By reaching out to him, we also take steps toward bettering our situation. Using our talents for good gives us genuine satisfaction and lets us serve him best. With that in mind, know that wealth is not the all-encompassing goal in life. Of course it isn't! Do not wear yourself out to get rich; have the wisdom to show restraint. It's written in Proverbs 23, and it's a salve for anyone who finds it difficult to calm down and let the future unfold with careful (not exhaustive) planning.

This wisdom has been shared for thousands of years, so let's take it to heart. Let's learn how to properly react when the market drops. Let's learn how to properly diversify that portfolio and use the proper tools. As we go on to further the holdings discussion in chapter 7, there's a steady truth to remember—whether you believe it or not.

Learn to set your goals wisely and to maintain your dreams, but always enjoy the journey. While learning the concepts of smart investing, remember that sometimes the most life-changing truths are deceptively simple. Onward to our discovery of the basic principles of equity holdings.

CHAPTER 7

Holdings: Smart Investing Simplified

In the last chapter, you learned that trying to beat the market is like showing up to a gunfight with a cap gun—you'll probably get wounded, and you probably won't win. To invest wisely, you need to work with the market instead of against it. In other words, you need to understand how the market works and play along rather than trying to beat it. This chapter will explain how by laying out a few basic principles and then combining them into an overall investment strategy. I'm grateful to Efficient Advisors for permission to use data, graphics, and information from their Advisor Resources presentation, Smart Investing Simplified (Efficient Advisors 2021).

The Jerusalem View

Ecclesiastes holds within it so many explanations for why diversification is a sound strategy in life. Here's one: "Ship your grain across the sea; after many days you may receive a

return. Invest in seven ventures, yes, in eight; you do not know what disaster may come upon the land" (Ecclesiastes 11:1–2).

Proverbs echoes the above by asserting that consistency is crucial, not a get-rich-quick mentality. "A faithful person will be richly blessed, but one eager to get rich will not go unpunished. . . . The stingy are eager to get rich and are unaware that poverty awaits them" (Proverbs 28:20, 22). Here we have yet more evidence that we want to avoid risky investments if we can't avoid the potential loss, as well as any investments whose losses could permanently damage our ability to amass wealth. When you do decide on an investment strategy and follow through with it, let go and trust that you've made a sound decision with the information currently available to you.

"My heart is not proud, Lord, my eyes are not haughty; I do not concern myself with great matters or things too wonderful for me. But I have calmed and quieted myself, I am like a weaned child with its mother; like a weaned child I am content" (Psalm 131:1–2).

The Main Street View

Main Street's view is all about action. What slinger weapon can we use to keep us competitive? Mark Twain has a great saying that illustrates the anxiety that can accompany this endeavor: "October is a peculiarly dangerous month to speculate stocks. The others are July, January, September,

April, November, May, March, June, . . ." You get the picture. How do we avoid this type of uncertainty?

It's time to look at the capital investment strategy that avoids speculating and is instead grounded in academic evidence. (Remember earlier in this book when I mentioned that Nobel Prize winners are much smarter than me? It's high time we all just went ahead and took their advice.) This academic evidence we'll examine is known as capital markets investment theory, and it's based on four components: structure and behavior, modern portfolio theory, an efficient market hypothesis, and the multi-factor model. Let's look at each of these four components to see how they can help us invest better, wiser, and with prudence.

1. Structure and Behavior Keys to Success

Yes, someone might occasionally beat the market through stock picking or security selection, or even market timing. But how's this for an argument against these three: Study after study shows that over 90 percent of a return comes from proper diversification, a concept we call "asset allocation."

In a landmark study, researchers Brinson, Hood, and Beebower discovered that a portfolio's performance hinged on the mix of assets or investments in said portfolio—not on stock picking or timing the market. Within the study, stock selection and market timing actually had a *negative* return on the portfolio (Brinson 1995).

Structure: the cost hurdle. Additionally, in terms of structure in asset management, cost can make a huge difference in returns. These costs are not always transparent. Yes, explicit costs are disclosed in a prospectus. These costs are publicly visible and include expense ratios, costs to run that money fund, mutual fund management fees, custodial fees, and trading costs. Those can really add up quickly. Then there are the nearly inevitable hidden or implicit costs, which are harder to calculate.

Here's a good example: Bid-ask spread costs are the implicit costs that result from mutual fund managers buying the underlying stocks in a mutual fund. Other implicit costs are referred to as turnover costs, and they can have a horrendous impact on a portfolio because they come out of the fund's return. If you think this isn't significant in terms of your possibility of a high return on investment, think again.

"The combination of commissions, the bid-ask spread, and market impact costs add up to at least 2 percent on average," says investment advisor and former economics professor Ron Ross (Ross 2002).

Mr. Ross, we're listening. Let's look in more detail at other elements that can keep us from amassing wealth when we "play" this unbeatable, unpredictable market.

Turnover. To get a better idea of the implications of turnover cost, one need only to look at recent percentages of available mutual funds. In data provided by Morningstar in 2020, turnover in US actively managed equity funds was 55 percent (Edelen 2013). That means, on average, active mutual fund managers buy and sell over half the stocks inside the mutual funds in the hopes of beating the market. We already know that this buying and selling activity ends up as a loser's game because the majority of active mutual fund managers tend to underperform the market over meaningful time periods.

Expense ratio. A further cost hurdle to overcome is the expense ratio cost. Since these costs are easier to calculate, it is important to understand the impact that expense ratios can have on an investment. According to Morningstar, the average equity mutual fund has an expense ratio of 1.24 percent. The 2020 ICI Factbook lists the asset-weighted average equity fund as 0.52 percent. It is my belief that you should buy only those domestic common-stock funds that charge close to a quarter of 1 percent (.25 percent) annually or less as management expenses.

Fees and trading costs. Additionally, though fees for investing in international funds tend to be higher than fees for US funds, it's wise to limit yourself to the lowest-cost index funds as well. You may also want to consider exchange-traded index funds, commonly known as ETFs. These are index funds that trade on the major stock exchanges and can be bought and sold like stocks. ETFs are available for broad US and foreign indexes and have some advantages over mutual funds. Often, they also have a lower expense ratio than index funds.

Cost differences can have a huge impact on a portfolio, and guess what? Cost is a guaranteed negative return. There is no such thing as "free" when it comes to this type of investing. It also doesn't make sense to pay for stock picking, market timing, sector rotation, or any other active management services for your investments that aren't likely to deliver your desired end result. Look at the evidence. Be wise in your decisions. You can hope to be an outlier, but the evidence doesn't lie.

2. Modern portfolio theory

The second part of capital markets investment theory is modern portfolio theory. Harry Markowitz, an economics professor, won the Nobel Prize in 1990 for this theory, which says it is possible to construct an efficient frontier of optimal diversified portfolios that offer the maximum possible expected return for any given level of risk (Markowitz 1952).

Modern Portfolio Theory

**Diversification works: Own multiple asset categories
that tend to have dissimilar price movements**

Goal: Maximize Expected Return
Given Level of Risk (Volatility)

Efficient Frontier

Risk-Free Asset

Expected Return

Harry Markowitz

1990   Nobel Peace Prize

1952   Portfolio Selection in
the Journal of Finance

Here's an easier way to think of modern portfolio
theory: diversify, diversify, diversify. It worked back in the
age of Solomon, and it works now. By diversifying a portfolio

with the highest expected return and lowest volatility risk, you can create an efficient investment strategy.

Here's a simple example of how an investment may actually give average returns that can be misleading. Look closely: Investment B gives you annualized growth that is a bit higher than that of Investment A, even though investment A has higher average annual returns. Advertising results can be misleading when variables such as standard deviation are not taken into account. In short, the volatility from period to period distorts the results. You're really seeking growth as the measure, not average returns.

This hypothetical is meant to educate you, but it may not actually reflect an existing mutual fund. It's just a representation of what I see time and time again.

What investment would you choose?	Investment A	Investment B
Average Annual Return	15%	12%
Standard Deviation	35%	15%
Annualized Growth %	5.49%	8.06%

How wonderful would it be to walk into the fortune teller's tent, ask what you should do with your money, and simply follow the advice to guaranteed success? Alas, that person does not exist. If you meet them, please grab a business card and email me their information. Because we cannot see the future, another part of our capital markets theory has to do with an efficient market hypothesis. This is another way of saying that no one has a crystal ball to predict the future of price movement. The actual prices visible today in the market reflect all the information we know about that particular stock. Only the currently unknown information we encounter tomorrow may change the price.

3. An efficient market hypothesis

This modern portfolio theory developed back in the 1700s. Remember sage Adam Smith? Well, he's back! We can trace the origins of this theory back to *Wealth of Nations* yet again. Smith discusses free markets as well as the impossibility of controlling both prices and information.

Borrowing from this belief, Louis Bachelier, a French mathematician and academic, wrote his PhD paper called *Theory of Speculation*. A lover of markets, Bachelier believed that markets are random.

Flash-forward to the 1930s, when Alfred Cowles, another economist and academic, became the first person to construct an actual index to compare how investment managers performed against said index. He believed it was possible to beat the market.

A few years later, Friedrich Hayek, academic and Nobel Prize winner, declared that the market itself was the best determinant of price and information. He had a deep impact on the next two academics who wrote prolifically about this matter. Paul Samuelson, an MIT professor, built on the work of prior economists and mathematicians to assert that market prices were random and unpredictable. This led to the work of Eugene Fama, who in 1965 wrote a paper called "A Random Walk and Stock Market Prices." Fama joined Samuelson's bandwagon. Market prices were random and unpredictable, he said, and that was that.

Efficient Market Hypothesis

Adam Smith
1700s

Louis Bachelier
1900s

Alfred Cowles
1930s

Friedrich Hayek
1940s

Paul Samuelson
1950s

Eugene Fama
1960s

Prices reflect information

All known, assumed, and speculated information is evident virtually instantaneously via price. It is highly unlikely that one investor can know more than the market does collectively.

Permission to use granted by Efficient Advisors from Smart Investing Simplified ©2022

What you see is what you get. That's really the efficient market hypothesis distilled from all the academic evidence: the prices we see today are all the known information we have about those stocks. Even if we try to predict the future, all we're doing is speculating. With more than 50,000 stocks in the market, we do know that mispricing occurs—but also that it doesn't occur in predictable patterns that can lead to outperformance. All this evidence goes to support the hypothesis that active managers cannot consistently add value to their stock picking and market timing.

Efficient Market Hypothesis

Mispricings do occur but not in predictable patterns that can lead to consistent outperformance.

Active management strategies cannot consistently add value through security selection and market timing.

Evidence-Based Investment Strategy: designed to reward disciplined investors with capital market returns.

Capital markets investment strategies are designed to reward the disciplined investor.

Since we know that efficient markets don't already have prices built into them, what evidence do we have that can help us get the most optimal return for our portfolio? For that answer, we turn to the multi-factor model.

Within this model, we're going to examine a concept called risk premiums in stock. We also want to take a look at the risk-free model, which we define as T-bills (Treasury bills).

Efficient Market Hypothesis

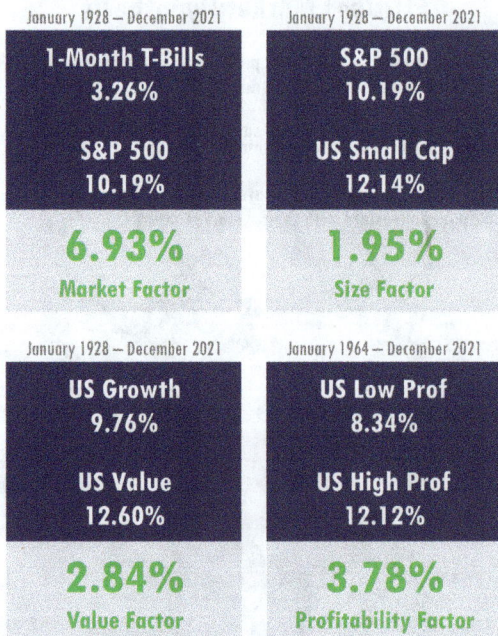

January 1928 – December 2021	January 1928 – December 2021
1-Month T-Bills 3.26%	**S&P 500** 10.19%
S&P 500 10.19%	**US Small Cap** 12.14%
6.93% Market Factor	**1.95%** Size Factor

January 1928 – December 2021	January 1964 – December 2021
US Growth 9.76%	**US Low Prof** 8.34%
US Value 12.60%	**US High Prof** 12.12%
2.84% Value Factor	**3.78%** Profitability Factor

Returns refer to the premium over the risk-free rate short-term treasury. Returns based on The Center for Research in Security Prices, University of Chicago. Data from 1/1928-12/31/2021 and 1/1/1964-12/31/2021. You cannot invest directly in an index. Unmanaged indexes do not reflect management fees, transaction costs, or other costs that are associated with some investments or a managed portfolio.

Permission to use granted by Efficient Advisors from Smart Investing Simplified ©2022

The one-month T-Bill will be the risk-free investment in our graph. You can always put your money there, and that's the return you'll see. Note: if we compare the S&P 500 from 1928 through December 2021, the difference is called the Market Factor premium.

Investing in the market gives you a premium over and above the risk-free investment rate (see Market Factor). Surprise: there are other premiums, and that's why we call it a multi-factor model. This next element to consider is that if we look at stocks from 1928 through December 2021, small stocks outperformed the S&P growth stocks (Market Factor) by close to 2 percent. We call that number the size factor premium. If you diversify further in your portfolio into what is sometimes called distress stocks or value stocks, this factor shows a close to 3 percent premium over the Market Factor.

The last category we'll examine using this model is the profitability factor. There are low-profitability stocks from 1964 to 2021 in our study, compared with high-profitability stocks. The comparison is a difference of over 3.5 percent. We call that the profitability factor.

Take this data from academic evidence to better understand how to diversify your portfolio. As I referenced earlier, 90 percent of your return comes from diversification. Through these premiums and these multiple factors, you can achieve a return that may exceed market averages through proper diversification. This is not guaranteed, but it does show potential probable outcomes. We'll go into more detail about how to do this later in the chapter by looking at a few portfolio examples.

4. The multi-factor model

The last component of capital markets investment theory is the multi-factor model. Let's examine this last capital market strategy as a means of diversifying. To do so, we're going to whittle down some of the factors we've already discussed to explain where investment returns come from and how you can structure a better portfolio. This is a theory that tells us you can structure your portfolio with three primary factors in mind to get optimal returns like Harry Markowitz's "efficient frontier."

As we noticed with the multi-factor model, if we compare the market to a fixed investment, such as Treasury bills, we tend to get higher returns over meaningful time periods by just being in the market. Generally, they outperform inflation over the long run. We have a fundamental decision to make when it comes to the right mix of stocks and bonds or fixed investments in our portfolio to outperform the market, with the given risk we're willing to take.

The second factor, the size factor, is also part of the multi-factor model. It asks, If we compare the largest stocks to the smallest in the US, which are going to have higher volatility? It's true that you have higher risk with the small stocks, and you also have higher volatility. Over time, though, the aggregate of small stocks generates a higher return when compared to just large stocks in your portfolio. What combination of large and small stocks will you select now that you understand this?

The third factor is value. It reveals that value companies tend to have a low stock price relative to the worth of their hard assets. When we compare their hard assets to their net worth, then, they could be considered unfavorable. Yes, sometimes these companies should be considered distressed or out of favor. However, if we examine the "stock universe," which would you expect to have a greater price volatility: the healthy (or somewhat healthy) companies, or the unhealthy ones? Data leads us, unsurprisingly, to the answer. So too does common sense.

Results indicate that you'll experience more risk in those value stocks. But sure enough, the data from more than five decades of research reveals that you get a higher return over time when you commit some of your stocks to the higher risk.

Finally, the most recent five decades of research indicate emphasizing High Relative Profitability along with the other three factors can further diversify stock exposures while pursuing potential returns.

Knowing how much exposure to risk-premium factors you can commit to over your investing lifetime is critical when you're making investment allocation decisions for your portfolio.

Capital Markets Investment Strategy

Building an Efficient Portfolio—60/40 Hypothetical Illustration: January 1999–December 2021

What do the graphics on the following pages of five portfolios tell us?

Let's bring it all together now: structure, modern portfolio theory, an efficient market hypothesis, and the three-factor model. It's time to apply these principles and build a diversified portfolio. We have the knowledge; now, let's act on it! We'll begin with Portfolio 1, the often-referred-to S&P Index, which consists of the five hundred largest publicly traded companies in the United States.

Portfolio 2: This is a simple index portfolio comprised of 60 percent S&P 500 and 40 percent bonds. If we take 40 percent of the stock out of Portfolio 1 and put it into bonds, what do you expect to happen to the risk? It goes down, right? Coincidentally, what happens to the return if the risk goes down? Sure enough, as you can see, the annualized return here is less than that of Portfolio 1 but still a respectable 7.15 percent.

Evidence-Based Investing Strategy

**Building an Efficient Portfolio—60/40 Hypothetical
Illustration: January 1999—December 2021**

Portfolio 1		Portfolio 2	
S&P 500	100.00	S&P 500	60.0
		Bonds	40.0

Annualized Return:	8.09	Annualized Return:	7.15
Standard Deviation:	14.96	Standard Deviation:	8.98
Growth of a Dollar:	$5.98	Growth of a Dollar:	$4.90

All US Equities (undiversified)   **Fixed Income Effect**

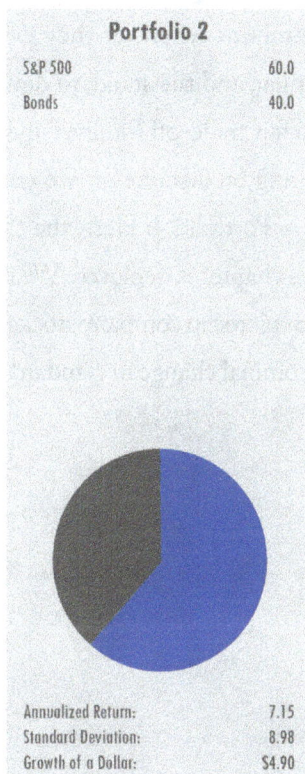

Permission to use granted by Efficient Advisors from Smart Investing Simplified ©2022

Portfolio 3: Let's look at what happens when we diversify the portfolio into international stocks and small stocks. The entire market capitalization of US stocks makes up only about half of the capitalization in free-trading stocks around the globe, so we should pursue equity market return premiums wherever they exist. The rate of return remains similar, and the standard deviation is slightly increased. This is a fair trade-off for diversifying globally rather than concentrating on just one or two countries.

Portfolio 4: Here, the third factor I discussed earlier in this chapter is deployed. We diversify even more in value and US microcap company stocks to pick up a bit more return for a nominal change in standard deviation. A sound strategy, yes.

Evidence-Based Investing Strategy-2

Building an Efficient Portfolio—60/40 Hypothetical Illustration: January 1999–December 2021

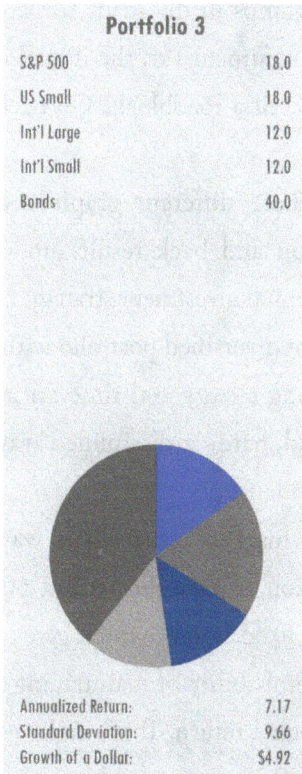

Portfolio 3	
S&P 500	18.0
US Small	18.0
Int'l Large	12.0
Int'l Small	12.0
Bonds	40.0

Portfolio 4	
S&P 500	10.0
US Small	8.0
US Lg Value	5.0
US SM Value	11.5
Microcap	1.5
Int'l Large	4.5
Int'l Value	4.5
Int'l Small	5.0
Int'l Small Value	8.0
Emerging Markets	2.0
Bonds	40.0

Portfolio 3	
Annualized Return:	7.17
Standard Deviation:	9.66
Growth of a Dollar:	$4.92

Global + Small Effect

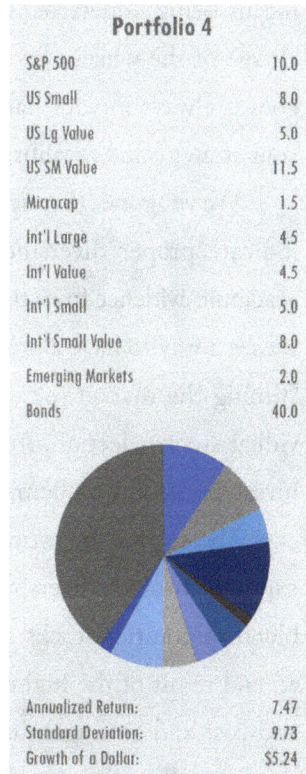

Portfolio 4	
Annualized Return:	7.47
Standard Deviation:	9.73
Growth of a Dollar:	$5.24

Global + Small + Value Effect

Permission to use granted by Efficient Advisors from Smart Investing Simplified ©2022

Adding value stocks means we can expect increases in the return for about the same risk. If I were a financial umpire, this is when I might yell, "Safe!"

No stock picking or speculation here. Friends, I can't say it enough: don't be stressed by the market. Having a plan means being undeterred by bumps in the road. You are in charge of the wheel of this investment car; the direction it goes is always in your hands. Hit a roadblock? Go back to your strategy and recalibrate.

We've gone through these different graphics that indicate proper diversification and back results up with academic evidence from the capital investment strategy. Now we see a way to have a prudent diversified portfolio without "timing the market" or wasting energy and time on individual stock selection. Instead, here's a disciplined way to invest, backed by academic evidence.

The capital investment markets are really a way to capture, through diversification, a portfolio with a 60/40 blend of equities/stocks and fixed/bonds, which gives you an end result of the highest probability of maintaining risk and cost and getting an expected return. That's right—you can have all of the above! In fact, we were able to capture nearly 92 percent of the "undiversified" S&P 500 portfolio return with approximately 35 percent less volatility. This is a fantastic way to understand the "risk story" and to hold on for a greater reward with higher returns over time.

Evidence-Based Investing Applied

Captured almost 92% of "Undiversified" All-US Stock
Return with 40% of the Portfolio in BONDS!

35% LESS Volatility (Risk)

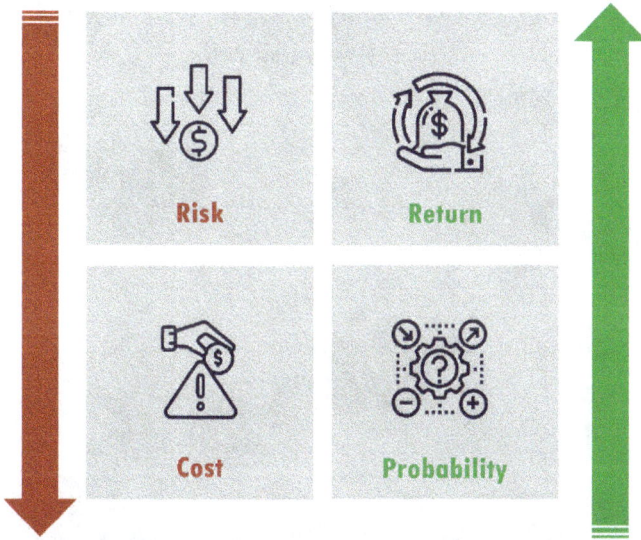

8.09% vs 7.47%

Permission to use granted by Efficient Advisors from Smart Investing Simplified ©2022

Don't be fooled into thinking you should invest solely in the S&P 500. You don't have to accept that volatility, so don't do it!

Let's take a peek at a portfolio of the S&P 500 by itself, with a hypothetical $100,000 invested. If we look at that investment over time and compare Portfolio 1, the S&P 500, to Portfolio 5, the small and value premiums in US and

OK with Higher "S&P" Volatility?

Why settle for undiversified, S&P 500 "only" returns?

January 1999–December 2021

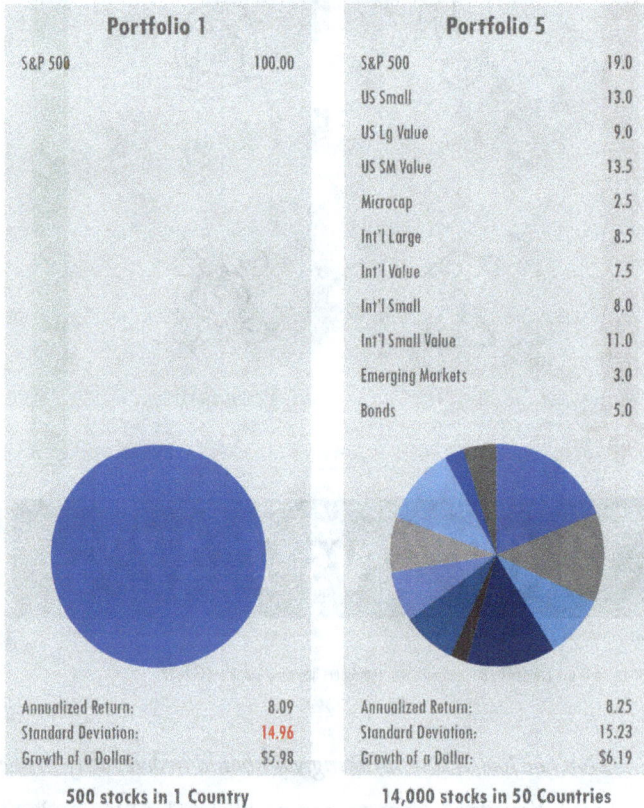

Portfolio 1	
S&P 500	100.00

Portfolio 5	
S&P 500	19.0
US Small	13.0
US Lg Value	9.0
US SM Value	13.5
Microcap	2.5
Int'l Large	8.5
Int'l Value	7.5
Int'l Small	8.0
Int'l Small Value	11.0
Emerging Markets	3.0
Bonds	5.0

Portfolio 1		Portfolio 5	
Annualized Return:	8.09	Annualized Return:	8.25
Standard Deviation:	14.96	Standard Deviation:	15.23
Growth of a Dollar:	$5.98	Growth of a Dollar:	$6.19

500 stocks in 1 Country   **14,000 stocks in 50 Countries**

International stocks actually yield greater opportunity than just holding the S&P over time.

If you want to just have equities and not do the bonds, compare these two and take to heart that diversification is your friend. Our last graphic in this chapter illustrates the Portfolio 5 yield for significant time periods is substantial. So, if you truly can tolerate holding as much volatility as a portfolio like the S&P 500, you might as well get paid for it.

OK with Higher "S&P" Volatility?

Why settle for undiversified, S&P 500 "only" returns?

Hypothetical $100,000 Portfolio Starting Value:

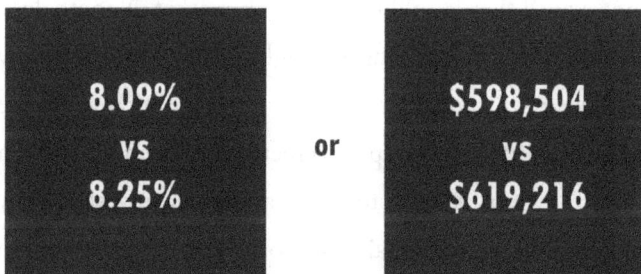

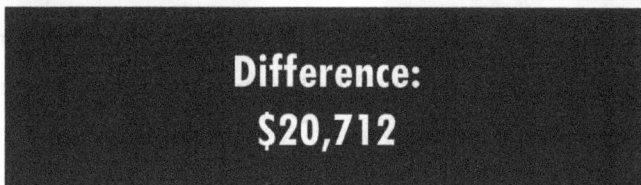

Permission to use granted by Efficient Advisors from Smart Investing Simplified ©2022

It's not that friend who calls you only when he needs something. No, this comparison is more akin to the friend who weathers the bumps and lumps of life with you. Over 90 percent of diversified portfolio returns do give investors returns and rewards over simply picking stocks.

The academic evidence shows active management lowers your probability and reliability. It also raises your costs. The efficient market hypothesis and modern portfolio theory provide greater returns than any of the "hot managers" out there over long periods of time. Diversification, discipline, and rebalancing are therefore your allies.

Before we leave this chapter, here's a final tool to add to your investment arsenal: self-directed private equity. This is not equity that is sold on the stock market. Nonetheless, private equity is increasing throughout the world in many portfolios even though it's not on a stock exchange. These may be limited partnership agreements that last ten to fifteen years, and you may have to be an accredited investor. They also require meeting legal costs to review any partnership agreements you enter.

I believe there's another way for the Main Street investor to look at private equity. Whether you do this inside your pension plan or outside, you can invest in real estate through self-directed investments. Investment advisors typically don't talk about self-directing largely because they're brokers.

Firms don't allow them to talk to you about self-directing in your IRAs and 401(k)s or in your Roth.

Still, you can get into these self-directed investments if they interest you, and one prime example in this category is real estate holdings. Take a moment and think about it. What strikes your fancy? Is it flipping properties, creating promissory notes, or some other non-publicly traded investment? I like real estate and equity indexes or ETFs in a portfolio. One way to build this up is through rentals. Through rental real estate, you can get tax-deferred growth and capital gains treatment upon sale.

Investigate how to get into these self-directed IRAs and 401(k)s. Many resources on the internet can educate you. And remember: even though the typical investment brokerage firm may not sell these or recommend them openly because they don't like these alternative strategies, they can be a great way for the average mainstream investor to diversify their portfolio and increase their net worth.

As with any investment option, a disclaimer exists. Each of these vehicles has its own risk and compliance issues. I encourage you to seek expert investing, legal, and tax advice before investing and to remember that everything taught in these chapters is not a guarantee. These are the musings of a financial advisor (me) who has experienced a good deal of success with certain modes of investing and less with others.

This book is educational and not meant to give specific investment advice. Seeking advice, knowledge, and wisdom is key, and we'll talk more about that in the next chapter.

CHAPTER 8

Pursuing Wisdom and Education

What we've learned thus far on our HERO Plan journey is that seeking wisdom is good for us. We're drawn to this journey toward answers. The human race doesn't leave most decisions to chance; we consider the positives and negatives of different strategies and choose the one that matches our situation best. Investing is no different. Here, we'll be combining Financial Commandments 7 and 8: We'll learn to seek wisdom in pursuit of financial abundance and financial peace. We'll also endeavor to seek education as a lifetime pursuit. The end of official schooling doesn't mean the end of learning!

Note that this chapter is short in comparison to some of the earlier chapters in this book. But as we know from mighty David, the smallest elements can prove to be the mightiest. The upcoming material is powerful ammunition for financial success; it also supports success in life in general. If we continually seek wisdom and education (understanding), the proper tools tend to present themselves.

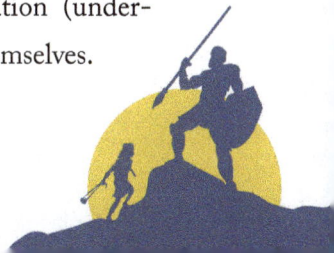

The Jerusalem View

The Book of Psalms and Proverbs teach us how to think; they also stress the importance of staying out of debt and cultivating good relationships. As we've discussed in other chapters, our interdependence as a species is needed on everyone's collective financial journey. We'll be examining that more in this chapter.

I encountered a very successful doctor years ago; let's call him Tom. He was meeting all of his financial goals and was very happy. Then Tom had an accident and could no longer practice surgery, which he described as his calling. This could have been the devastation of his life. Instead, through wisdom and his education, Tom knew he had other gifts from God to share with humanity. He changed course in his professional life and became a renowned professor.

Tom couldn't follow his original passion of conducting surgery anymore. And just as investors must come to terms with long-held investment advice that isn't working for them, he needed to pivot to achieve future success. It's tough to give up something that you believe in. If it's not working for you, though, revisit your inner tally of God-given gifts. Seek the counsel of those who share your values, whether in the investment arena or the tax, legal, or insurance sectors. And, yes, in life in general. Surrounding yourself with like-minded people who want the best for you? It's a no-brainer.

"Plans fail for lack of counsel, but with many advisers they succeed" (Proverbs 15:22). In Proverbs, we learn that plans often fail when we don't consult wise and knowledgeable people, but with many sound advisors backing those plans, they tend to triumph. Yes, it's a tried-and-true idea to enlist fellow travelers on your life's journey. Those who subscribe to your own value system are worth their weight in gold. Surround yourself with people who believe what you believe and genuinely want you to flourish.

"Blessed is the one who does not walk in step with the wicked or stand in the way that sinners take or sit in the company of mockers, but whose delight is in the law of the Lord, and who meditates on his law day and night" (Psalm 1:1–2). We need to seek God's understanding and wisdom. It should come as no surprise that this journey is both never-ending and occasionally uncomfortable. Many of us would rather not spend the extra time it takes to acquire wisdom and true understanding, but that's a recipe for a life lived on the surface. It has no substance or meaning. That's not to say that wealth building need be a slog! Remember how I talked about finding joy in financial classes as I pursued what I ultimately deemed my calling in life? Seek balance in your life in all pursuits, and throughout it all, remember the true meaning of our existence: to serve others with our God-given talents and abilities and, by doing so, to glorify Him.

As a society, we are too often out of balance as a people of extremes. We borrow, spend, and work excessively during our early years, and then want to quit altogether during the golden era. Why not keep learning? Keep trying? Seeking to better our lives is admirable, no matter if you're one year old or one hundred years old. And though there is time for harder work and time for rest, finding peace throughout the journey is paramount.

"You who are simple, gain prudence; you who are foolish, set your hearts on it" (Proverbs 8:5). To continue on your financial independence journey, you're going to need to figure out how to serve God by serving others. You also need to believe that your time to flourish is coming. That's the mindset we're going to talk about here, and it's from the vantage point of a mentor or leader. Ultimately, life is not about you and what makes you comfortable. It's about how you can act as a leader who serves others through your God-given talents and abilities. Also, just because we haven't yet "hit it rich," and even though we may want to seek recreation and retirement, God reminds us that there's a season for everything: "There is a time for everything, and a season for every activity under the heavens: . . . a time to tear down and a time to build, . . . a time to be silent and a time to speak" (Ecclesiastes 3:1, 3, 7).

The Main Street View

Be a mentor—and surround yourself with mentor leaders.

Examining the Main Street view, it seems a good time to introduce you to one of my mentors who continues to exert great influence in my life. I first shook Manny Ramos's hand over thirteen years ago. A former marine drill instructor turned personal trainer, Manny has that "special something" that draws people to him. He's a fitness coach, counselor, mentor, and nutritionist, among other titles. Through him, I continue to witness firsthand that when God gives you certain gifts and you surround yourself with like-minded people, you get results. No, I'm not training for any muscle-building competitions anytime soon. But Manny helps me become my best, healthiest self.

It's not just your financial advisor who is important in helping you to craft a healthy, robust life journey. Look to your pastor, CPA, and, yes, even your favorite trainer for guidance. These people examine the short and long run of your decisions and have your best interest in mind. They understand that people make mistakes—and then they help you move past them.

I'll never forget the words motivational speaker Zig Ziglar had to share about this topic. In the book *Born to Win*, Ziglar proposes that the more knowledge one possesses about a subject, the better equipped one is to link daily experience to new opportunity. These are the people who see possibility around every corner.

As a young man seeking Main Street wisdom, I also gained deep insight from observing John Wooden, the "Wizard of Westwood." As an iconic basketball coach, he won twelve NCAA championships. He achieved seven of these victories consecutively, and his feat has been unmatched in any sport.

He wasn't a man with a singular focus, though. Wooden helped his students become successes on *and* off the court. Throughout all of this, he always referenced a principle called the Pyramid of Success. The pyramid, comprised of fifteen

Pyramid of Success

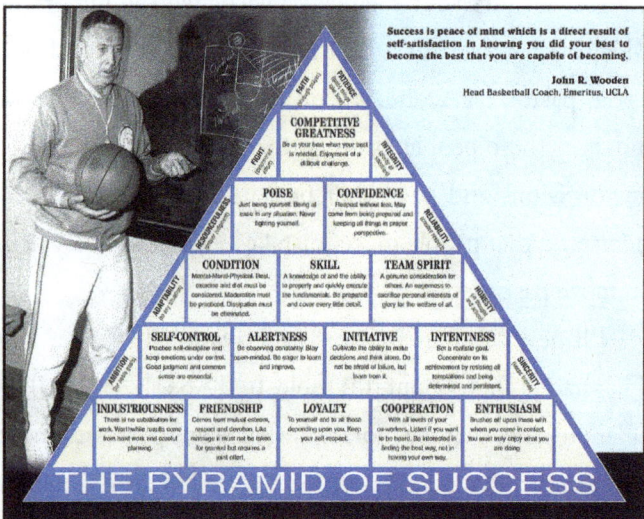

attributes that include initiative, skill, condition, and enthu-siasm, plays a pivotal role in levels of success.

At the base of the pyramid sit five characteristics that form the basis of all our successes and comprise all the wisdom and knowledge we create in life. No shock here: they're rooted in hard work. Look closer, and individual attributes emerge: industriousness, friendship, loyalty, coop-eration, and enthusiasm. Anyone can choose to emulate these behaviors. You don't have to be a savant or have some special talent to begin developing these characteristics or traits. Isn't that refreshing?

The next step of the pyramid includes self-control, alertness, initiative, and intentness. Again, these are traits anyone can embody. If you possess a beating heart, you can climb this pyramid, so to say, to success. How do you know when you've arrived at the peak? John Wooden says that success itself is peace of mind, a direct result of satisfaction in knowing you made an effort to be the best you can be. This definition is simple. It's attached to elements you can control. It's about the effort, not the outcome—the journey, not the destination.

No external factor can change the fact that you put forth real, intentional effort in your life. Still, too many people attach success to a material object or outcome. Phrases like *I'll have made it when I have* _____ and *I'll have more time when I reach* _____ are too prevalent in our society. Yes, striving is good. But life is unpredictable. If your definition of success is one thing and you don't achieve it, are you a failure?

Let's ask that question another way. Did Dr. Tom's inability to operate on patients make him useless? Absolutely not. He took what he could control and made the best situation out of it he possibly could. During this financial peace journey, nothing is guaranteed. All you can do is work with the tools you've identified that are best for you and hope for the best.

"The only thing in your control is effort. That's all and that's everything," Mark Cuban once said (*Business Insider* 2012). As a multifaceted businessman, he hit the proverbial nail on the head. The key to success is to focus on what is in your control and to do those things to the best of your ability. John Wooden's words about character further this notion of focusing on what you can actually do instead of focusing solely on the end result. Focus on your character, he says, more than your reputation. While reputation is simply what others say you are, character is what you are. Be the best you can be, he urges, and don't care what anyone else thinks.

This isn't just self-help poster material. Having a pure character and striving for success for the right reasons means that once you achieve success, you'll find it easier to maintain. Ability may get you to the top, Wooden cautions, but it takes character to keep you there. Focus on that. Meditate on what comes from within. That's really the key to any successful

Financial Ten Commandments teaching here in this book. Consider your mental and moral qualities—what's within you. Once you've mastered those, you can go after any goal with gusto.

Improving those qualities helps us reach our own personal definitions of success, and there are varying ways to sharpen these tendencies. One way is to consider the books we read; according to Matthew Kelly, reading is to the mind what exercise is to the body—and what prayer is to the soul.

The world of learning has really expanded since the days the encyclopedia salespeople made the rounds of the neighborhood. Now, answers are available with a single click. Podcasts distill topics down to easily digestible nuggets we consume while commuting or jogging down the street. Never before in the annals of human history has it been so possible to become the best versions of ourselves, knowledge-wise.

Besides having exposure to many schools of thought, we are also living in an age that doesn't subscribe to the idea that success is predetermined. According to Professor Carol Dweck in her mindset book, we can learn to fill our potential. Instead of believing we are born with certain skills and traits that can be limiting, she encourages people to overcome this fixed mindset (Dweck 2008, 141). A fixed mindset doesn't grow, expand, or seek wisdom. Instead, she says, subscribe to the growth mindset strategy. Always be learning, seeking, and expanding.

That concept radiates outward and influences those you surround yourself with. Think about the people whose advice you value most. Some you've likely gleaned from thanks to their ability to quickly acquire knowledge; others you may be blessed enough to know personally. Part of a growth mindset is keeping your mind open to those who give wise counsel and help you thrive in knowledge.

"Knowledge has to be improved, challenged, and increased constantly, or it vanishes," said Peter Drucker (Ziglar 2017, 79). We need to consider ways to help others develop and stop expecting natural competence in every situation. If you're a boss, for example, think about how you can begin seeing and treating employees as collaborators. Create a culture of self-examination, open communication, and teamwork. Everyone has natural predilections. Remember, at the beginning of the book, when we said to find something you enjoy and pursue it? Doing so doesn't mean you'll be an expert. Seek the advice of those who make you better. And don't expect others to be perfect either.

Surrounding yourself with people who point out your blind spots and help you grow is also essential. I've been blessed in my career to work with my daughter, Christie, who helps me create a culture of self-examination and communication among my team. The constructive criticism and coaching we provide each other as co-leaders is priceless.

We make each other better by becoming better both independently and as a team.

Learning from others and collaborating with them is part of the human interdependence we talked about in chapter 3. Another part is being generous with your wealth for others' benefit, and we'll turn to that in the next chapter.

CHAPTER 9

Growing a Generous Spirit

Throughout my years as a financial planner, I've been blessed to associate with many clients who believe that sharing God's wisdom is their true meaning in life. These people include gems like my client Deborah (not her real name), who brought me gifts from Israel after each of her annual pilgrimages. She did this for nearly a decade, knowing I cherished these items. One such gift is a breathtaking wine cup and saucer used in the Jewish Havdalah service.

During this service, which is performed at the end of each week on the Sabbath, Jewish families pray and sing to God to ask him to bless the upcoming work week. The wine is then poured into the cup to symbolize the material blessings of the family. Memorable, right? The ceremony doesn't stop there. The wine continues to be poured and overflows onto the saucer. This visible metaphor of "sharing the wealth" and "my cup over" is a consistent reminder to me that I am here on this earth to bless others, not just myself. It is a beautifully

pure demonstration of what we are supposed to do for each other as fellow humans.

I keep that cup and saucer near my desk as a daily reminder that I'm called, as we all are, to give not only of our material blessings but also of our time, attitude, forgiveness, love, and compassion. Everyone's cup of blessings is different, and God will use our talents and abilities according to his will. Our job is to recognize and enjoy the fruits of our labor as we fill our own cup, making sure it is sufficient for our own household. As it overflows, we are called to bless others.

Even when there aren't extensive riches to share, that overflow may be visible. My mother, Shirlee, lived by this selfless principle. I didn't fully know this until her funeral, when a woman approached me to share that my mother would periodically bring her gifts "just because." The woman assumed she was rich because the gifts were sometimes lavish. That surprised me. My mom was a widower. She didn't have much for herself, and she definitely did not have a huge sum of money stocked away to share with others. She lived modestly, and though she never considered herself poor, she didn't have a lot of money in the bank.

She could have held tight to the little surplus she did have, fearing that she wouldn't have enough to live on in her later years. Instead, she was generous with her gifts. As you can imagine, I teared up when I heard this story, as I do whenever I recall it. My mother knew the true meaning of abundance. She was a blessing to all around her.

The Jerusalem View

The example of how Shirlee lived her life is timely. Generosity is the financial commandment of this chapter, and I ask you to really consider what that word means to you. Generosity is not necessarily about tithing, though supporting the church is an admirable pursuit. Financial Commandment 9 is more in line with my mom's giving spirit, and it's a lesson for the rest of us. Take stock of your very existence. What did God make you to be? What resources have you been blessed with? Whether it's your time, talent, or treasure, share as much as you can, as the scripture tells us in the following verses.

"Whoever is kind to the poor lends to the Lord, and he will reward them for what they have done" (Proverbs 19:17).

"Honor the Lord with your wealth, with the firstfruits of all your crops; then your barns will be filled to overflowing, and your vats will brim over with new wine" (Proverbs 3:9–10).

To be very clear, this book does not support the idea of prosperity theology, in which God automatically rewards righteousness with material wealth. Jesus would have been the richest man in the world if that were true! Plenty of good people fall on hard times. Also, wealth is transient.

In Proverbs, we find Biblical acknowledgment that wealth doesn't last forever.

The concepts in the HERO Plan and the Financial Ten Commandments teach that prosperity is a matter of personal responsibility, hard work, diligence, and perseverance. A strong work ethic and other entrepreneurial traits, such as initiative and perseverance, are critical to a life of economic prosperity. They don't guarantee it, but they definitely do help.

Why do we care so much about our downtrodden brethren? Wouldn't it be more primal for us to be self-serving? Thankfully, it's not. God's compassion for the poor is clear throughout the Book of Psalms and other writings in scripture, and many people feel called to help those less fortunate.

As we are now armed with what Jerusalem has to say about generosity, let's turn our focus to Main Street tools. Welcome to another slinger weapon I call the HERO Charitable Trust.

The Main Street View

Let's begin with a case study—a story about a successful businessman I worked with who grew his business over the course of four decades. Throughout his lifetime, I observed him earning about a million dollars each year from the endeavor. Still, his operations always funded more than just his family lifestyle. They also funded his holdings and the investments of others. He lived within his means and invested the surplus. After forty years, he was ready to sell the business. He had by then amassed a $40 million gain. That's a pretty good end number—but how much would he ultimately get to keep?

If done traditionally, the sale would likely result in about half that amount going toward taxes. After paying off debt, he would be left with perhaps 20 percent of that $40 million. That's a lot less than the impressive number he had expected to fund the whole next phase of his life. There had to be another solution!

Together, he and I sought wise counsel and financial advice, and the tool we ultimately discovered was what I call the "wealth-builder's special weapon": the HERO Charitable Trust. This trust is a weapon that can beat those financial giants, helping you to meet your goal of keeping that hard-earned money and sharing it the way you choose. By paying a smaller share of taxes, you can have more freedom to be generous with your wealth. You can also make sure your family is well taken care of when you plan your estate. The revocable living trust and the HERO Charitable Trust are the subject of the next chapter.

CHAPTER 10

Planning for the Future

The first trust to understand is the revocable living trust. The R in the HERO Plan stands for revocable living trust (RLT). Not only does it help the greater good for your family, heirs, and those you love, but this type of trust also:

1. Allows you to set up provisions for minor children or a dependent with special needs to help manage their affairs.

2. Allows you to avoid probate, which is important when you own real estate or a business.

3. Along with other estate documents (durable power of attorney for health care, will, and others) lays out a plan to your heirs for settling or passing on your estate at your death (Kohler 2017, 272).

More than 50 percent of Americans don't even have a will, much less any of the other documents mentioned

to assist your heirs with your estate. My advice, seek legal counsel immediately to plan and implement your estate.

The HERO Charitable Trust

An explanation of the HERO Charitable Trust deserves a chapter all its own. Trust me, I want to shout the news about this trust from the rooftops. In my many years of practice as a financial advisor, I've seen this arrangement serve clients to better manage the tax impact of large capital gains looming from a business or real estate sale. It makes me excited to tell you about it now. When people look to shed the burden of managing highly appreciated assets, such as business holdings or real estate investments, it's here as a viable option.

Full disclosure: this option is not for everyone. For one thing, it's expensive. When you set up one of these trusts, make sure to seek proper legal and financial counsel. I suggest that shooting for perhaps $5 million in gains and upward would make financial sense for you. I do believe it's for many who have enjoyed the fruits of their prosperous businesses and highly appreciated real estate. I'm not downplaying outright selling and giving to charity, but for many, the tax hit is just too much. They want another solution.

If your advisors have never heard of this type of charitable trust, this section will definitely give you food for thought before you pay Uncle Sam the large gains on your real estate or other highly appreciated assets as stock in your business. Let's take a look under the hood, as they say, to see what challenges this trust can solve. Can you tell I'm passionate about this?

Many people I have counseled throughout the years realize they have amassed a good deal of wealth in their real estate equity. The tax code is actually their friend when it comes to selling their home with a personal tax exemption. At the time this book was written, that can amount to $250,000 per person or $500,000 per married couple tax-free. It's also known as IRS Code Section 121, and it's a blessing, to be sure. But what about the rental real estate gains or the business building?

If you have large taxable gains, the following strategy may be your answer to saving on taxes and, at the same time, creating cash flow for your HERO Plan. It also supports your favorite charities at the end of the trust term.

What is a standard charitable remainder trust (CRT)? The CRT is a split-interest trust where you own property donated to the CRT and receive income for an initial period of time. After that initial interest terminates, the "remainder" that is left in the trust goes to a predesignated charity, the remainder interest. Through careful planning, the right kind of legal support, and advice from those who understand the myriad of tax implications, it can be a powerful tool for many reasons. Some of these are tax savings, cash flow, asset protection, and selfless giving at the finish line (Kohler 2019,

191). If you don't outlive the lifespan of the CRT, your heirs will be living out your values of giving and supporting those charities. This robust CRT for higher-capital-gain property is the HERO Charitable Trust, and it lives up to its HERO adjective (Wilson 2023).

- It's a great 1031 tax-free exchange alternative. There's no 45-day identification period, no 180-day "gun to your head" to close on replacement property, no requirement to purchase, and no time limitations on reinvesting your sale proceeds.
- This type of CRT allows you to invest in anything you choose. If, for example, you don't want to own rental property anymore, and that's been a main source of income for you thus far, you don't need to continue.
- What if your partner wants to separate and therefore you are unable to do a 1031 exchange to solve the tax deferral? Each partner can defer tax on their respective gains independent of the other using this CRT.
- Don't leave your children with property to fight over—use the CRT to defer tax and create a separate fund for each child. It also allows you to develop a wealth plan for each child during your

lifetime that is tailored to the child's risk profile and investment preferences.

- Those who wish to sell some of their properties and then purchase a single large property or dream home can do that through this CRT, which allows you to sell multiple properties over time and defer the tax on each or combine the untaxed sale proceeds to purchase any asset of your choice. It also gives you a long-term strategy for disposing of your real estate portfolio tax efficiently.

- This CRT lets you sell appreciated property and defer the tax on the gain or wait as long as you wish to identify and purchase replacement property (as mentioned above, without any of the 1031 constraints). Unlike a traditional 1031 that requires carryover basis, it allows you to get a full step up in basis on the new replacement property.

- If you want to keep a property in your family for generations but don't want to pay the estate taxes, this CRT strategy allows you to keep the property in the family while minimizing the estate tax.

Sign me up, but only after careful review and consultation with a law firm that is experienced in implementing this strategy.

If you've paused mid-highlighting to suddenly wonder why the HERO Charitable Trust is so seldom discussed and taught to tax professionals, here's my take. It's a nontraditional structure. This cash flow, tax, and giving strategy allows you, as I've detailed, to give a modest amount to charity at the end of the beneficiary's life or twenty or more years later at the end of the trust (this makes you the hero of this story).

Here's the hidden secret of the HERO Plan: you get to take the tax deduction for the remaining interest today, not *forty years in the future* when the remainder defaults to charity! This is a slinger weapon indeed, and a perfect time to pivot as we close this chapter with a quote from the Book of Psalms.

"For the Lord God is a sun and shield; the Lord bestows favor and honor; no good thing does he withhold from those whose walk is blameless" (Psalm 84:11).

As we have done throughout this book, we'll look at views from Jerusalem and Main Street in this chapter. But first, I want to check in with you. How are you feeling about your ability to use the knowledge in this book as a slayer tool to vanquish those giants keeping you from financial prosperity? We're almost through our journey together, and I sincerely hope you're feeling more in control of your wealth-building destiny with each passing page.

The Jerusalem View

Did you know that the Old Testament describes sons as having received their inheritance while the father was still living? The patriarch was then able to oversee the son's stewardship while he was alive. This reminds me of the care we need to take when developing our own plans for succession.

I have too often encountered cautionary tales during which estate planning has been a disaster. One woman in particular comes to mind. Perhaps you know someone like Sue, who thought she was doing the right thing when she hired a "trust mill." Sue's heart was in the right place, as they say. However, she ultimately created a trust without using an attorney. The trust company had limited authority, and they never actually put the assets into a trust at all. They never changed the title to any of the assets.

She passed away believing that she had done everything she could to secure her wealth for her child, who would be taken care of after her death because she had prepared. The trust she had set up was not valid, though, so her son had to drive hours back and forth to local courts for six months. The case became stuck in hearings, and the stress of trying to sort out the legality of the inheritance was too much for him. He suffered a heart attack.

Sue's is just one brief story of many, and as I mentioned before, I have unfortunately been privy to others. Avoid the same fate by reaching out to a competent law firm with experience dealing with estate and trust planning. No, I'm not giving legal advice in this book. I just want to make sure you understand the overall idea of what you should be doing to secure your wealth. Hopefully, I've helped you avoid a situation like what Sue's son went through. The way you leave your wealth to your heirs will have a significant impact on them.

Just like those Biblical fathers did with their real-time succession, you should be involved in your estate plan. Communicate your values to your progeny. Who are you as a person, as a parent, as a member of the family? How do you hope they will continue your legacy? There's a spiritual component to this, as most of this book alludes to. This isn't an arbitrary idea. As Christians, our material aspirations should be rooted in the spiritual. If you plan to make your children significantly wealthier, make sure that you also take significant time to instill in them concepts like those I've shared throughout this book.

Verbalize your values while you're living. Teach your heirs to be productive citizens of humanity, not just consumers. Will they create joy with their riches, or will they squander the opportunity? The spiritual inheritance you leave behind can be the fertilizer that enriches your family tree for generations to come.

Taking a page from the Biblical forefathers, consider giving some assets away early—before you leave this earth. Doing so will assist your heirs with this training process. Also, be aware that passing an entire estate on to your children may not be wise in all cases. Refer back to the HERO balance sheet goals in chapter 2, where we discussed the need to build social and spiritual capital. Instill these concepts in your children *before* the financial windfall. They then can pass the concepts on to their children. "Wisdom, like an inheritance, is a good thing and benefits those who see the sun. Wisdom is a shelter as money is a shelter, but the advantage of knowledge is this: Wisdom preserves those who have it" (Ecclesiastes 7:11–12).

The Main Street View

Let's examine the words of Socrates as we move on to the Main Street view of perpetuation of wealth. The philosopher said that if he could get to the highest place in Athens, he would lift up his voice and say, "Fellow citizens, why do you turn and scrape every stone to gather wealth and take so little care of your children to whom you must one day relinquish it all?"

A "Jerusalem meets Main Street" view that echoes what we see in scripture is a story I'll share of one of my good friends, Larry Hoekman, who was the pastor at my daughter's wedding. He wrote a book on how to embark on intentional grandparenting with God's vision. Larry suggests we reflect on our legacy by asking, "At your funeral, what do you want your grandkids to remember about you?" Our words to our children and grandchildren about caring for others and giving from abundance don't seem to mean as much as our actions. A good action step to reflect on the legacy you're leaving would be to write your own epitaph. Those words on your tombstone sum up who you were on earth (Hoekman 2021, 82).

So go ahead—write it. This is the essence you want to pass on to your children and grandchildren. Will it say, "I built wealth and gave it away without a thought to where it would go and who it would help"? Or will it declare, "I used the wealth I amassed on Earth for good, and instructed my children to do the same"? It's up to you.

Now it's time for some more soul-searching. What amount do you believe God wants your estate to grow, and why? What is your vision for its ultimate distribution? These are important questions. When you evaluate your estate plan, vividly understand what you want to accomplish so you know when you've arrived at that goal. Otherwise, you'll always wonder whether you've forgotten some pertinent detail.

There are only a few options you have in dealing with your estate, though there are many ways to do each one. You're giving your money either to family and friends or to charity. Some might go to the government in the form of taxes, and some might go toward legal costs. It's imperative that you plan the allocation of the money and assets you've collected throughout your lifetime. I recommend that you spend some time in prayer and contemplation as you seek the wisdom of God in this answer.

Also, and I can't say it enough: work with a competent attorney who specializes in estate planning. Don't leave this important job to a paralegal or trust mill. Yes, there are plenty of online programs that purport to do this service; don't trust those either. Now, let's talk about charitable giving as part of your estate legacy.

Earlier in the chapter, I mentioned that charitable giving can be accomplished through the estate plan. In larger states, it's sometimes difficult to eliminate the large estate tax liability without the use of the CRT vehicle. Another consideration is the allowance for liquidity. This can provide financial flexibility as needed during a transition period, which is right after someone has passed away.

Having some money available to whoever is going to handle your estate is important, because it will take legal help to have assets transferred and titled and retitled. Some sort of liquidity should be available for access, whether that's in the form of savings or perhaps a life insurance policy. This also assists in preventing the quick sale of your non-liquid assets in unfavorable economic climates.

Don't make it difficult for your heirs to carry out your wishes. Instead, prepare them with the financial cushion they need to wade through the intricacies of your estate. Help them avoid having to make any rash decisions because of financial constraints.

I've often dealt with estates that take a long time to prepare inherited real estate for sale. No one wants to be stuck having to liquidate those kinds of assets quicker than necessary. You want to facilitate estate tax payments and make it easier to distribute the assets among your heirs, but you also want to make it easy to manage your estate administration.

My advice is to use the RLT as a vehicle, as I mentioned at the beginning of this chapter. The trust provides for the management's distribution of assets over a period of time. When you pass away, you want to distribute the assets to the beneficiaries, according to the trust instructions, as soon as administratively possible. This can help avoid the probate costs that often accompany a will. It's also an effective tax planning tool.

Consult your tax advisor and attorney regarding the advantages of a trust, which typically involves three parties. The trust, or grantor, sets up this legal contract. The assets then pass to your beneficiary, the one who will receive your assets. The third party is the trustee, the person who is going to read your trust and make sure it is carried out in accordance with your wishes.

There are many different types of trusts. I won't give you an exhaustive list here (you're welcome), but know this niche can be complicated and difficult to navigate. Within this chapter, I really want to emphasize the importance of the R in the HERO Plan, and that's the RLT. Meet with your estate attorney to construct the type of trust best suited for your estate and charitable living goals.

The RLT can be dissolved or amended at any time as long as you're alive and deemed competent. It also provides a degree of privacy with regard to the distribution of your estate assets. Additionally, it provides an ongoing management structure for the trustee to effectively administer the distribution of your estate as you desire.

Many of my clients have had their own HERO Plans in place for decades. Knowing that they will act as stewards in their next phase of life allows them to take care of their family and financial goals first while also helping others. The HERO Plan answers the question of how to access as much of your money as possible throughout your lifetime while also supporting the charities you believe in and the family you want to keep secure. Let's work on your HERO Plan in the next chapter.

The House of_____

Operations

_____

_____

_____

Holdings

_____

_____

_____

_____

H.E.R.O.

Eliminate Reductive Debt

_____

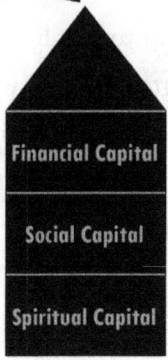

Financial Capital

Social Capital

Spiritual Capital

Revocable Living Trust
Yes/No
Date Created _____

*Inspired by Mark J. Kohler

CHAPTER 11

Happiness, Stewardship, and Our Calling

Let's bring our HERO Plan together now as we combine holdings, elimination of reductive debt, a revocable living trust, and effective operations. To help you on your way, I have a worksheet for you to complete on the previous page. This HERO Plan is blank on purpose—copy it, tear it out and write on it.

I'd like you to begin by just jotting down some notes. Perhaps you've been doing this as you've been reading, or maybe you're more of a highlighter aficionado. Whatever works for you!

On that worksheet, you'll be asked to declare your "house." Mine is the House of Benedetti. Proudly write your name in that space. It represents what you're compiling for the good of your family, your friends, and society at large. Then, take a breath and consider the role of free-market capitalism in this whole wealth-gaining endeavor. It's pretty amazing!

Next, consider your Operations where capitalism is an important tenet of your wealth-building program. History shows us that the best system to take care of our families, our own self-interest, and the needy is this free-market capitalist system. Capitalism also provides the resources necessary for either private charity or public assistance (through taxes).

This in turn helps the poor. Both charity and government assistance assume productive wealth creation. No one claims capitalism is without flaws or limits; the system is simply the most consistent way to bring out the best in people. That's one reason I often look to Adam Smith and his ideas on free-market development. His declarations give me peace that I'm on the right track in amassing wealth. Your own HERO Plan will harness capitalism to promote the common good, including that of your descendants.

The history of the development of capitalism shows us that rather than limiting and defining people according to the socioeconomic class in which they were born, it presents every individual with opportunity. Upward mobility is possible. Capitalism has brought with it an unprecedented transformation of the world's social fabric. It brings us together and breaks down social barriers. It unites people with a common form of commerce. Today, more than any other time in the history of humankind, social classes around the world intermingle in the open marketplace of free enterprise.

You are a part of this symbiotic system because your participation in the capitalistic free-market enterprise requires cooperation. People come together: rich, poor, middle class, well educated, and poorly educated. All of us work in tandem to accomplish common objectives. As we discussed throughout this book, one of the most remarkable things about capitalism is the degree of cooperation required of otherwise self-interested individuals. It helps the whole.

As you develop your HERO Plan, ruminate on the unifying force of capitalism across all ages of humanity. Jonathan Pennington wrote that there is nothing so natural and inescapable as a desire to live—and to live in peace, security, love, health, and happiness (Pennington 2015). The desire to see humanity flourish motivates everything we humans do. All human behaviors, when analyzed deeply enough, will be found to be motivated by the desire for life and individual advancement.

Combining the Jerusalem and Main Street Views

Let's pivot once more to Jerusalem's view as we ponder what Solomon has to say in Ecclesiastes. We understand innately that no two human beings are the same. We are as unique as our fingerprints. Still, all hearts share the same intrinsic desire. We are all created in the image of God with a desire to know him and to flourish, whether we acknowledge this or not. This universal truth has been written in our hearts and is part of our nature and design. As such, it transcends trend, culture, and time. As Solomon wrote, "He has made everything beautiful in its time. He has also set eternity in the human heart; yet no one can fathom what God has done from beginning to end" (Ecclesiastes 3:11).

The idea of human flourishing is the Old Testament concept of shalom that I described in chapter 4 about our interdependence as humans. We also seek peace of mind in our financial life, Shalom is the Hebrew word that means "peace" (Lapin 2010, 118). Shalom means universal flourishing and wholeness—a rich state of affairs in which needs are satisfied and natural gifts fruitfully employed; shalom, in other words, is the way things ought to be. It is the full flourishing of human life in all aspects, as God intended.

This full flourishing is made possible through the HERO Plan. Through our operations and holdings, we can bring to fruition the potential that has always been within us.

For the Main Street view on this subject, let's look to the words of Nobel Prize winner Daniel Kahneman in his book *Thinking, Fast and Slow.* The general accepted measure of happiness, he purports, is a question you address to your remembering self. When you are asked to think about your life, answer this question: "All things considered, how satisfied are you with your life as a whole these days?" (Kahneman 2011, 391).

How do *you* answer this question? Similar self-reflection is routinely used in large-scale national surveys worldwide. Since this is a book focusing on the financial independence journey, I'll summarize some of the findings from Kahneman's book as they relate to financial satisfaction and how they vibe with your HERO Plan.

It's a mistake to believe you will experience greater well-being purely from the pursuit of wealth. After a certain point, when all of your basic needs are met, well-being does not continue to increase. Money buys happiness, but only to a point. A 2010 study by Kahneman and August Deaton found that having more money was associated with better emotional well-being. Hooray, one might think: the pursuit of wealth is worthy in its own right! Well, not always. The study found that after a certain point (income of about $75,000 per year), satisfaction levels drop rapidly.

When those basic needs of housing, nutrition, and health care are met, the happiness gain of earning more money becomes smaller (though wealth level does add to life expectancy). Money might not make you exponentially happier, but it may lead to deep levels of satisfaction if you look to use your wealth in certain ways.

Here's where things get interesting. Instead of asking people if they are happy and comparing those answers to income levels, a new survey by the Robert Wood Johnson Foundation asked respondents about their life satisfaction.

As it turns out, happiness has a "satiation point" that trails off even for those who have more money. However, life satisfaction continues to rise with income through at least the $500,000-per-year threshold (Robert Wood Johnson Foundation 2020, 6).

Whether that number is truly $75,000 or $500,000, I suspect that everyone's going to have their own level at which happiness is not satisfied anymore by just the things you can buy with money. I estimate that there are subtle differences between members of the monied set and everyone else, including control of their time and schedule, a sense of optimism for their children, and an expectation that their assets will give them options in a changing environment.

The bottom line is this: money is a tool. It can buy you control and give you more time. It creates options. We shouldn't be surprised that (at least up to a point) more money leads to greater life satisfaction. There's a clear contrast between the effects of income on experienced well-being and on life satisfaction as a whole. Higher income brings with it greater satisfaction, well beyond the end of its positive effect on experience. The general conclusion is that a person's evaluation of their life and their actual experience may be related, but they are also different.

The Best Use of Your Resources

To find personal fulfillment, don't just look to a balance sheet. Throughout this book, we've examined different weapons or tools that can slay the financial giants keeping you from attaining meaningful wealth. Discern your calling as you develop your plan for economic flourishing, and then, just as David used his slinger weapon to slay the mighty Goliath, knock those roadblocks down.

As we've undertaken our journey toward building meaningful wealth, we've looked to the HERO Plan as a way to expand investments and passive income. We expanded the HERO model itself with the Financial Ten Commandments. And we dove into these in depth as we compared Jerusalem's view with Main Street's.

As I close this book, I hope you understand that greater economic and life nourishment is best accomplished if it glorifies God. He tasks us with caring and cultivating this creation of Earth. What an honor to be part of God's perfect work! My hope for you is that you meld your relationship to economics and practice what God commands, which is wholehearted stewardship. Stewardship is all that we have and all that we are. Every second of our time is a gift from God.

The word *stewardship* comes from the Greek word *oikonomia*, a Greek compound word translated as "the management of household affairs, stewardship, and administration." To be effective stewards, we must be wholehearted in our dedication to God's purposes. God is not asking us to be a steward of part of our income, talents, and time. He asks us to steward all of it. The Hebrew scripture sums it up well: "Hear, O Israel: The Lord our God, the Lord is one. Love the Lord your God with all your heart and with all your soul and with all your strength" (Deuteronomy 6:4–5). This commandment is known as the Shema, which means "hear." Making decisions and hearing God's calling pleases God in our role as stewards.

This book is fundamentally about hearing God's calling for your life and acting as the steward of the resources you create. These resources are economic choices. We are called to do well with the limited time, talent, and treasure we have and create.

No matter who you are or what God has called you to, your job is to do it well. When you think this way, you'll count the costs and consider the outcomes. My prayer is that you'll have more profit left over with which to serve God's creation. This world is His, not ours. He gives us a job that we must do in a way that meets His standards. In doing so, we please and glorify Him.

REFERENCE LIST

Augustine. 1995. *The Works of Saint Augustine: A Translation for the 21st Century: Sermons.* Hyde Park, New York: New City Press. https://wesleyscholar.com/wp-content/uploads/2019/04/Augustine-Sermons-341-400.pdf.

Brinson, Gary P., Randolph L. Hood, and Gilbert L. Beebower. 1995. "Determinants of Portfolio Performance." *Financial Analysts Journal* 51 (1): 133-138.

Blodget, Henry. 2012. *Mark Cuban: There's Only One Thing in Life You Can Control: Your Own Effort.* Business Insider, January 1. https://www.businessinsider.com/mark-cuban-theres-only-one-thing-in-life-you-can-control-your-own-effort-2012-1#.

DALBAR. 2021. "DALBAR Study finds the Average Investor Return Gap Doubled in 2021." August 25, 2021. https://www.dalbar.com/Portals/dalbar/Cache/News/PressReleases/2021QAIBMidYearPR.pdf.

Dweck, Carol S. 2008. *Mindset: The New Psychology of Success.* New York, New York: Ballantine Books.

Edelen, Roger, Richard Evans, and Gregory Kadlec. 2013. "Shedding Light on 'Invisible' Costs: Trading Costs and Mutual Fund Performance." *Financial Analysts Journal* 69 (1): 33-34.

Efficient Advisors. 2021. *Smart Investing Simplified.* Philadelphia, PA: Efficient Advisors, February 1: 33. http://www.efficientadvisors.com.

Garrigou-Lagrange, Reginald. 1948. *The Three Ages of the Interior Life: Prelude of Eternal Life,* translated by M. Timothea Doyle. Vol. 1. St. Louis, Missouri: B. Herder Book Co. https://www.ecatholic2000.com/lagrange/interior1/interior.shtml.

Hoekman, Larry. 2021. *Intentional Grandparenting with God's Vision.* Nipomo: A Silver Thread.

Kahneman, Daniel. 2011. *Thinking, Fast and Slow.* New York: Farrar, Straus and Giroux.

Kohler, Mark. 2017. *The Business Owner's Guide to Financial Freedom: What Wall Street Isn't Telling You.* Irvine, CA: Entrepreneur Press.

—. 2019. *The Tax and Legal Playbook: Game-Changing Solutions to Your Small-Business Questions.* 2nd ed. Irvine, CA: Entrepreneur Press.

Lapin, Daniel. 2009. *Thou Shall Prosper: Ten Commandments for Making Money.* 2nd ed. Hoboken, NJ: John Wiley & Sons.

Luckey, William R. 2017. *Wealth Creation: The Solution to Poverty.* Grand Rapids, Michigan: Acton Institute.

Markowitz, Harry. 1952. "Portfolio Selection." *The Journal of Finance* (Wiley) 7 (1): 77-91. http://www.jstor.org/stable/2975974.

Pennington, Jonathan. 2015. "The Universality of Human Flourishing." *A Biblical Theology of Human Flourishing* (Institute for Faith, Work & Economics) 22. https://tifwe.org/resource/a-Biblical-theology-of-human-flourishing-2/.

Ramsey, Dave. 2021. *Baby Step Millionaires.* Franklin: Ramsey Press, The Lampo Group, LLC.

Robert Wood Johnson Foundation. 2020. *Life Experiences and Income Inequality in the United States.* Harvard, Boston: T.H. Chan School of Public Health, 95.

Ross, Ron. 2002. *The Unbeatable Market: Taking the Indexing Path to Financial Peace of Mind.* Eureka, CA: Optimum Press.

Smith, Adam. 2023. *The Wealth of Nations.* S&P Global. New York, New York: Bantam Dell a Division of Random House.

SPIVA. 2021. "SPIVA U.S. Year-End 2020." https://www.spglobal.com/spdji/en/spiva/article/spiva-us-year-end-2020/.

Wilson, Reg. 2023. *One Pagers.* Los Angeles, CA, January 31.

Wimmer, Brian R., Sandeep S. Chhabra, and Daniel W. Wallick. 2013. "The Bumpy Road to Outperformance." Valley Forge, PA: The Vanguard Group.

Ziglar, Zig and Tom Ziglar. 2017. *Born to Win: Find Your Success.* Issaquah, WA: Made for Success Publishing.

ABOUT THE AUTHOR

TRENT BENEDETTI is a Certified Public Accountant and Certified Financial Planner. But these licenses and training didn't protect him from being broke and the related financial stress. It was taking a toll on his married life, too, until Barbara, Trent's wife, and he took the Dave Ramsey Financial Peace course in 2010. The FPU class began Trent's journey to understanding financial peace concepts from a Biblical perspective.

In this book, Trent shares with you over forty years of wealth-building knowledge and financial peace principles that he uses in his tax and financial planning practice. The Financial Ten Commandments distills the concept to help you develop your own plan, Trent calls your HERO Plan, toward financial wealth building from a Biblical perspective.

Along with his training and education as a CPA and CFP, Trent has also completed the Main Street Tax Pro

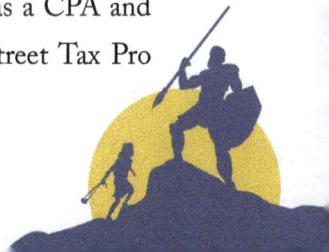

certification program offered by Mark J. Kohler and the Financial Coach Master Training program offered by Dave Ramsey. Integrating these Main Street programs with a Biblical perspective led Trent to obtain a Masters Degree in Biblical Theology.

The tools and principles learned in Trent's over 40 years of experience and hardship changed the trajectory of Trent's financial peace journey. These same tools are offered in this book, *Slay Your Financial Giants.*